*Law*Basics

EC LAW

SECOND EDITION

AUSTRALIA
Law Book Co.
Sydney

CANADA and USA
Carswell
Toronto

HONG KONG
Sweet & Maxwell Asia

NEW ZEALAND
Brookers
Wellington

SINGAPORE and MALAYSIA
Sweet & Maxwell Asia
Singapore and Kuala Lumpur

*Law*Basics

EC LAW

SECOND EDITION

By

Janet B. Paterson, B.A., LL.B., Dip.L.P., LL.M.

Lecturer, School of Law, Napier University, Edinburgh

THOMSON ™

W. GREEN

Published in 2004 by

W. Green & Son Ltd
21 Alva Street
Edinburgh EH2 4PS

www.wgreen.co.uk

Printed in Great Britain by Creative Print and Design (Wales) Ebbw Vale

No natural forests were destroyed to make this product;
Only farmed timber was used and replanted

A CIP catalogue record for this book is available from the British Library

ISBN 0414 01576 2

NOTE TO SECOND EDITION

This second edition has taken into account amendments to the EC Treaty made by the Treaty of Nice 2000 in the light of future enlargement of the Union to 25 Member States in May 2004.

New competition rules (entering into force May 2004) have also been included, as have cases decided in the Court of Justice to update all other matters of Community law covered by this modest volume.

Janet B. Paterson   January 2004

CONTENTS

TABLE OF CASES

ix

TABLE OF EQUIVALENCES

Previous Numbering	New Numbering
Title I	Title
Article D	Article 4
Article F	Article 6
Title II	Title II
Article G	Article 8
Title V	Title V
Article J.3	Article 13
Title VI	Title VI
Article K.7	Article 35
Part One	Part
Article 1	Article 1
Article 2	Article 2
Article 3	Article 3
Article 3b	Article 5
Article 4	Article 7
Article 5	Article 10
Article 6	Article 12
Article 7 (repealed)	—
Part Two	Part Two
Article 8	Article 17
Article 8b	Article 19
Part Three	Part Three
Title I	Title I
Article 9	Article 23
Chapter I	Chapter 1
Section 1 (deleted)	—
Article 12	Article 25
Article 15 (repealed)	—
Article 16 (repealed)	—
Article 18 (repealed)	—
Article 28	Article 26
Article 29	Article 27
Chapter 2	Chapter 2
Article 30	Article 28
Article 31 (repealed)	—
Article 32 (repealed)	—
Article 33 (repealed)	—
Article 34	Article 29
Article 36	Article 30
Title III	Title II
Chapter 1	Chapter 1
Article 48	Article 39
Article 49	Article 40
Article 50	Article 41
Article 51	Article 42

Chapter 2	Chapter 2
Article 52	Article 43
Article 53 (repealed)	—
Article 54	Article 44
Article 55	Article 45
Article 56	Article 46
Article 57	Article 47
Article 58	Article 48
Chapter 3	Chapter 3
Article 59	Article 49
Article 60	Article 50
Article 66	Article 55
Chapter 4	Chapter 4
Article 70 (repealed)	—
Title IV	Title V
Article 75	Article 71
Title V	Title VI
Chapter 1	Chapter 1
Section 1	Section 1
Article 85	Article 81
Article 86	Article 82
Article 89	Article 85
Article 90	Article 86
Section 3	Section 2
Article 92	Article 87
Article 93	Article 88
Article 94	Article 89
Chapter 2	Chapter 2
Article 95	Article 90
Chapter 3	Chapter 3
Article 100	Article 94
Article 100a	Article 95
Title VI	Title VII
Chapter 1	Chapter 1
Article 103	Article 99
Chapter 2	Chapter 2
Article 107	Article 108
Article 108	Article 109
Article 108a	Article 110
Article 109	Article 111
Title VII	Title IX
Article 115	Article 134
Title VIII	Title XI
Chapter 1	Chapter 1
Article 117	Article 136
Article 118	Article 137
Article 118a	Article 138
Article 118b	Article 139
Article 119	Article 141
Article 120	Article 143
Article 121	Article 144
Article 122	Article 145

Article 190	Article 253
Article 191	Article 254

1. INTRODUCTION

Students approaching European law may be forgiven for feeling confused about what exactly they are studying. The law of the individual Member States that make up the European Union? The law of the European Union as a whole? The law of the European Community? Or Communities? And what is meant by "The Treaty"? Clarification of terms is certainly required.

The term "European Communities" refers to the European Coal and Steel Community (ECSC) established in 1952, the European Atomic Energy Community (Euratom) and the European Economic Community (EEC) both established in 1958. These were set up among the six founding Member States. When referring to "the Community" it is this latter Community, the EEC, which is generally meant. This is why "Community" in the singular is mostly used. To complicate matters, the Treaty on European Union (the Maastricht Treaty) in 1992 changed the name "European Economic Community" into "European Community" (EC). The contents of this study guide are those areas of law and policy dealt with by the European Community.

The European Union on the other hand, was established among the (by then) twelve Member States by the Treaty on European Union (TEU) and marked "a new stage in the process of creating an ever closer union among the peoples of Europe". It did not replace "the European Community" which remains a separate entity within the European Union. The TEU added new fields of activity and processes to the original Treaties setting up the three Communities (above). The European Union is founded on three elements, or "pillars":

- The European Community;
- A Common Foreign and Security Policy; and
- Police and Judicial Co-operation in Criminal Matters.

This small volume is concerned with European Community (EC) law. It is the law within the Member States, but not the laws of the Member State. To begin at the beginning...

THE EUROPEAN UNION

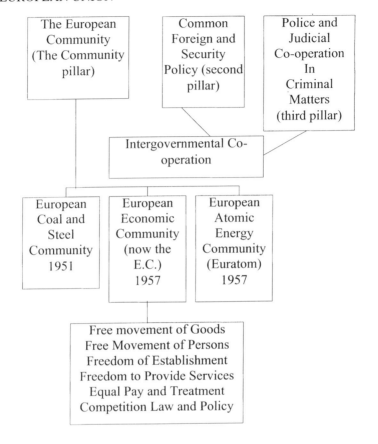

2. FROM COMMUNITY TO UNION

The establishment and development of the European Community took place against the backdrop of conflict between European nation states. Incessant warfare had resulted in such devastation that by the late 1940s it was clear that it was no longer possible for nation states, particularly those European powers who still ruled over large colonial empires, to operate political and economic policies which did not involve their immediate neighbours. At the same time, apprehension over the ambitions of the Soviet Union which by that time had occupied the Eastern part of Europe impelled the democratic states of Western Europe and the United States of America to join in the North Atlantic Treaty Organisation (NATO).

Although reconstruction of post-war Europe was under way by the end of the decade, aided in no small part by millions of dollars poured into Western Europe by the United States by way of grants and loans under the Marshall Plan, the threat of Soviet expansion prompted moves towards the creation of some form of mutual interdependence. The French statesmen, Jean Monnet and Robert Schuman devised a plan for a partnership between France and Germany for the production of coal and steel within the framework of an organisation open to the participation of the other countries of Europe. The Schuman Declaration was adopted on May 9, 1950 (a day now celebrated within the Member States as "Europe Day"). In 1951 the Treaty of Paris was signed, bringing a European Coal and Steel Community into being in April 1952. It was anticipated that not only would this pooling of the entire European coal and steel production under an independent authority eliminate the potential for conflict between France and Germany but would provide a sound basis for economic unification and expansion in the future.

The founders of the ECSC used the word "supranational" in the original Treaty to describe this independent authority. Although the Community had been created through an international treaty concluded between sovereign nations, the signatories were aware that they had created something very different from simply another international organisation. Not only did they accept mutual obligations, but they limited their own sovereign rights, transferring some of them to independent institutions over which they had no direct control and conferred on these institutions powers which they themselves did not possess. A legal system had been created to which the words "international" and "national" did not apply. The term "supranational" indicated that difference.

The European Coal and Steel Treaty then set up four institutions. These were based not on a rigid separation of powers, but on a community of interests. These institutions were:

- A High Authority formed by independent appointees of the Member States' governments, with responsibility for taking legally binding decisions and running the new Community. This body would act in the Community interest;

- A Council of Ministers made up of one representative from each of the Member States to represent the interests of those Member States (the signatories to the Treaty);
- An Assembly with delegates appointed by their respective nations' parliaments to represent the interests of the peoples of Europe; and
- A Court of Justice which would adjudicate on disputes and review the legality of the acts of the High Authority.

The signing of the European Coal and Steel Treaty in Paris on April 18, 1951 by the six founding countries (France, Germany, Italy, Belgium, Netherlands and Luxembourg) may be regarded as a first step towards European integration. Subsequently a European Atomic Power Community (Euratom) was created by the Treaty of Rome signed on March 25, 1957. The intention was to create a specialist market for atomic energy, distribute it throughout the six countries who had signed the ECSC and sell on surpluses to non-Member States. Euratom shared the Assembly and Court of Justice with the ECSC but had its own Commission (similar in nature and functions to the ECSC's High Authority).

In 1956, "The Six" had also begun negotiations to set up another Community dealing with a wider range of economic matters. A second Rome Treaty signed on the same date as the Euratom Treaty brought the new Community into effect in 1958. It was entitled "The European Economic Community" (EEC). Its whole raison d'être was to establish and ensure the effective functioning of a Common Market based on free and fair competition and the abolition of trade barriers and as its preamble stated, "to lay the foundations of an ever closer union among the peoples of Europe". While the EEC had its own separate Commission and Council of Ministers it shared the Assembly and Court of Justice with Euratom and the ECSC.

In contrast to the other two treaties, which as "traités loi" specified the exact powers of the Institutions, the EEC treaty was a "traité cadre", a framework Treaty setting out general principles, leaving it to the Institutions to work out policy and the detailed measures necessary to implement such policy. The initial steps towards achieving the goal of an efficient and effective Common Market involved the establishment of a customs union eliminating all customs duties and quotas between Member States and the creation of a common customs tariff for goods arriving from other non-Member States.

The aspirations of the founders were quite clear. They included:

- The formation of a supranational organisation;
- The creation and maintenance of a tariff-free market; and
- The development of a programme which would lead to the removal of all other national economic barriers throughout Europe, sector by sector, leading to deeper economic integration and one from which it would only be a short step to eventual political union.

A Customs Union became fully operative by 1968. This meant that tariff and quota restrictions to trading between Member States had by then been abolished and that the replacement of national external tariffs by a common external tariff had been completed. However, by 1969 full freedom of movement had not yet been achieved in the markets for goods, persons, services and capital. Nor were the Community's Institutions as effective as had been envisaged; decision making and legislation were taking place all too slowly. Throughout the 1970s there was pessimism about the future of the EEC. Economic crises on a global scale as well as internal political difficulties within the Member States of the Community had weakened the resolve of its members to press on with further integration.

In 1985 several crucial events occurred which added impetus to the integration process. On January 1, Jacques Delors was appointed as the new President of the European Commission. With his encouragement, the UK Commissioner (Lord Cockfield) produced a detailed White Paper on the internal market which set the date of 1992 for elimination of the remaining barriers to trade. As the European Community could only act within the limits of the powers conferred upon it by the Treaties (which the Member States had signed and ratified) further modifications to its powers could only come about through amendment to these Treaties by way of Intergovernmental Conferences (IGCs) of the Member States. Despite opposition from some Member States, an IGC took place, the outcome of which was the Single European Act of 1986. This Treaty, ratified by all Member States was the single most important amendment to date of the EEC. It was comprised of two parts relating to its internal and external components. Its main features were to speed up the creation of a European economic market without internal frontiers and to reform all the main Institutions of the Community to make them more effective, efficient and democratically accountable. This was to be achieved by:

- Inauguration of the internal market programme which was to be completed by December 31, 1992;
- Replacement of unanimity by qualified majority voting within the Council of Ministers for two-thirds of the 300 measures identified in the Cockfield White Paper as necessary to complete the internal market;
- Creation of a co-operation procedure allowing the European Parliament enhanced participation in the legislative process by giving it a second reading of proposals;
- Formalisation of the European Council (previously known as Summit Meetings between Heads of State and Government) as an organ of the European Community with increased policy-making authority;
- Recognition of the Assembly as the European Parliament;
- Creation of the Court of First Instance to ease the workload of the European Court of Justice;
- Co-operation in an economic and monetary policy;
- Common policy for research and technological development, and environment protection; and
- harmonisation in the areas of health, safety, consumer protection, professional and vocational qualifications, public procurement, VAT and excise duties, and frontier controls

The second part of the Single European Act contained provisions for European Political Co-operation—that is, foreign policy co-operation between governments. The Act rekindled enthusiasm for integration within Europe and acted as a stimulus to accelerate further integration.

As a result of this renewed enthusiasm for integration, an IGC was convened and on February 7, 1992 the Treaty on European Union (TEU or "the Maastricht Treaty") was signed by the 12 Member States. It brought into being a new legal entity—the European Union. Of the three pillars of the European Union created by the Treaty, the first and—for our purposes—most important, was the European Communities pillar. This was composed of the three Communities which were established in the 1950s; the European Economic Community (EEC), the European Coal and Steel Community (ECSC) and Euratom. The other two pillars related to a Common Foreign and Security Policy (covering the political aspects of foreign policy as opposed to the economic aspects which are still within the Community pillar) and Justice and Home Affairs (now, since the Treaty of Amsterdam in 1997, called Police and Judicial Co-operation in Criminal Matters). These latter two pillars involve intergovernmental co-operation only.

As well as setting out a framework for the respective competences of the component parts of the Union, one of the central tenets of the Treaty was to set out detailed provisions for the organisation of Economic and Monetary Union (EMU) and a timetable for its realisation.

Modifications were also made to the EEC Treaty (which was renamed the EC Treaty) to amplify Community powers in some areas, attack what was widely perceived as a democratic deficit, strengthen the powers of the Institutions and redress what appeared to be a widening gulf between the Community and its citizens.

The Treaty on European Union:

- Set out a common institutional framework for all three pillars of the Union;
- Introduced the principle of subsidiarity to its law-making process;
- Created the status of Citizen of the European Union;
- Introduced new, modified and expanded powers in the areas of economic and social cohesion (aid to less well-off regions), environmental protection, research and technological development, consumer protection, vocational training, the establishment and development of trans-European transport networks, public health protection, culture and development co-operation;
- Changed the rules on the appointment of the Commission;
- Introduced a third reading stage for the European Parliament by way of a new co-decision procedure and extensions of the previous procedures;
- Created the position of Ombudsman;
- Introduced enhanced participation in European affairs by a Committee of the Regions; and
- Created sanctions in the form of fines and/or periodic payments which could be levied by the Court of Justice in the event of a Member State failing to comply with its Community obligations.

The law contained in the (amended) EC Treaty within the Community pillar is still referred to as EC Law or Community law.

After complex negotiations during its passage and some considerable delay in ratifying it within the Member States thereafter, the Treaty on European Union entered into force in November 1993.

The reforms agreed at Maastricht were widely perceived as disappointing and disillusionment with Europe was increasingly reflected in public opinion. In particular, the unity of the Community system seemed to be threatened by the provisions allowing for flexibility of Member States' action which allowed for the possibility that only some Member States would participate in certain policies with others deciding to proceed at a slower pace—if at all. Examples of this were the UK opt-out from the Social Policy chapter and the UK and Danish option to decide later whether or not to join the Economic and Monetary Union. Accordingly the issues involved were quickly revisited and in 1996 a further IGC was convened with the aim of "ensuring the effectiveness of the mechanisms and the institutions of the Community". To some extent, progress was made:

- Some matters relating to visas, asylum, immigration and other policies relating to the free movement of persons were to be incorporated into the Community pillar instead of being located in the third pillar where they were the subject only to intergovernmental co-operation procedures;
- That third pillar was to be renamed Police and Judicial Co-operation in Criminal matters;
- Agreement on institutional reform to provide for enlargement did not materialise. Instead, the main points agreed were that Parliament's powers would be strengthened;
- Some Member States were to be provided with the means to move to closer integration between themselves in certain specified areas;
- Acts of the Institutions could be reviewed by the Court of Justice to ensure their compliance with the principle of respect for human rights;
- Provision would be made for legislation to combat discrimination; and
- Political control over a Member State guilty of certain serious and persistent breaches would all be incorporated in a new treaty agreed by all existing Member States.

On May 1, 1999 the resulting Treaty of Amsterdam came into force. The existing Treaties were then amended accordingly (see *Appendix 1*, p.106). This involved not only altering their content, inserting new provisions and repealing old ones, but also re-numbering most of the previous provisions.

In this respect great care requires to be exercised in identifying the correct Article of the Treaty. In the consolidated version of the Treaties published by the Office for Official Publications of the Communities, each Article is referred to by its new number first, with the previous one in brackets. This is the approach taken throughout this book. However, all legislation and cases delivered before the Treaty of Amsterdam entered into force refer to the old numbering scheme. In such cases, the citation will read, for example Article 30 (now Article 28). In addition, the content of some Articles has also been repealed, expanded or otherwise changed. Where possible, notation to this effect has been included in the text. For assistance in this "simplification" of the Treaties, a Table of Equivalences has been included.

One of the most important issues which had in effect been postponed during the IGC, surfacing only in one of the Protocols to the Treaty of Amsterdam and several Declarations to the Treaty was reform of the Union's institutional structure in preparation for eastward enlargement. At the

European Council's Cologne meeting in 1999, a further IGC was called which through the Treaty of Nice 2000 brought the following provisions into effect on February 1, 2003:

- As from January 1, 2005 the Commission shall include one national of each of the Member States—reducing the five larger Member States' representation from two to one. If and when the Union consists of 27 Member States, the number of Commissioners shall be less than the number of Member States. This number will be set by the Council of Ministers acting unanimously, chosen according to a rotation system based on the principle of equality, and will take into account demography and geography;

- The President of the Commission will receive increased powers concerning internal organisation of the Commission;

- Votes in the Council will be re-weighted. In addition to meeting the threshold for a qualified majority vote, the Treaty stipulates that a vote in the Council will require the support of a majority of Member States and that a Member State can request verification of whether the majority vote represents at lease 62 per cent of the total population of the Union;

- Extension of qualified majority voting in the Council in a number of policy fields will be extended resulting in a decline in the necessity for unanimity;

- Extension of the co-decision procedure for law-making within the Community will take place, giving increased authority and responsibility to the European Parliament;

- there will be an increase in size of the European Parliament to a maximum of 732 MEPs and it will be placed on an equal footing with the Council and Commission with regard to the instigation of proceedings under Article 230 (see Chapter 7, Judicial Review)

- The Council of Auditors will be composed of one representative from each Member State;

- There will be an increase in size of both the Economic and Social Committee and the Committee of the Regions to 350 members each;

- Within the Court of Justice there will be increased use of chambers and a redistribution of responsibilities between it and the Court of First Instance:

- Enhanced co-operation between Member States will be provided for; and

- Three competences have been added to the powers of the Union:

  1. the establishment of Eurojust, a unit of public prosecutors to co-ordinate the fight against crime (Article 31 TEU);

  2. a provision to combat fraud on the public finances (Article 135a EC); and

3. social exclusion and modernisation of social security systems are added to the objectives of social policy (Article 137 EC).

Today there are two Communities (the ECSC expired in July 2002) comprising 15 Member States, now known collectively as the European Union. These are "The Six"' who have been joined over the last 40 years through Accession Treaties by the UK, Denmark and Ireland (1973), Greece (1981), Spain and Portugal (1986) and Austria, Finland and Sweden (1995). In October 1990 German reunification took place. The German Democratic Republic joined the Federal Democratic Republic of Germany, bringing a further 18 million people into the Union. By virtue of the Merger Treaty of 1965, the Communities share the same institutions as does the European Union under its common institutional framework. These institutions remain legally independent although their powers are derived from their respective Treaties (ECSC, Euratom and EC Treaties). Since 1979, representation in the European Parliament has been by direct vote, rather than appointment from national parliaments.

It is expected that in the period up to around 2010, some 12 more Member States will be added to the European Union mainly from Central and Eastern Europe. From 1 May 2004, ten countries will join the Union: Cyprus, the Czech Republic, Estonia, Hungary, Latvia, Lithuania, Malta, Poland, Slovakia and Slovenia. The Accession Treaty for these ten new Member States was signed in Athens in April 2003, adding 75 million people to the population of the Union. Under their agreements with the European Union, applicant countries have undertaken to fulfil stringent criteria for membership. These specify that the applicant country:

*   Has achieved the stability of institutions guaranteeing democracy, the rule of law, respect for human rights and the protection of minorities;
*   Has a functioning market economy as well as the capacity to cope with competitive pressures and forces within the union;
*   Has the ability to take on the obligations of membership, including the "acquis communautaire". This term refers to all principles, policies, laws, practices, obligations and objectives that have been decided and agreed upon since the establishment of the original Communities, whatever the form in which it was done, whether legally binding or not. In other words, it refers to the body of rules that govern the Communities in all their fields of activity; and
*   Adheres to the aims of political, economic and monetary union.

At the European Council's meeting in Laeken in December 2001, it was decided to establish a Convention on the Future of Europe, with Valéry Giscard d'Estaing, a former French President as its chairperson. The Convention consisted of 113 representatives. Its main purpose was to debate the future of the Union and the adoption of a European Union Constitution, particularly:

*   Simplifying the treaties—reorganising the basic provisions of the present treaties into a single treaty;
*   Setting out the powers of the Union with particular emphasis on the principle of subsidiarity;

- Considering of the status Charter of Fundamental Rights of the European Union; and
- Clarifying the role of national parliaments within the institutional structure of the Union.

However, at the Brussels meeting of the European Council in December 2003, under the Italian Presidency, consensus on the form of a final document could not be achieved and at the time of writing, the Irish Presidency of the Union (lasting from January 1, 2004 until June 30, 2004) has announced its intention of pressing forward with the tasks of the Convention with a view to reaching agreement between the current 15 Member States and the 10 countries which will be joining the Union in May 2004.

---

3. SOURCES OF INFORMATION

TEXTBOOKS

A.M. Arnull, A.M. Dashwood, M.G. Ross, and D.A. Wyatt, *Wyatt & Dashwood's European Union Law* (4th ed., Sweet and Maxwell, 2000)

P. Craig and G. de Burca, *EU Law—Text, Cases and Materials* (3rd ed., OUP, 2003)

K Davies, *Understanding EU Law* (2nd ed.,Cavendish Publishing, 2003)

J. Hanlon, *European Community Law* (3rd ed., Sweet and Maxwell, 2003)

T. Kennedy, *Learning European Law* (Sweet and Maxwell, 1998)

P. Kent, *Law of the European Union* (3rd ed., Longman, 2001)

J. Steiner and L. Woods, *Textbook on EC Law* (8th ed., OUP, 2003)

J. Tillotson and N Foster, *European Union Law: Text, Cases and Materials* (4th ed., Cavendish Publishing, 2003)

S. Weatherill, *Cases and Materials on EC Law* (6th ed., OUP, 2003)

C. Vincenzi, and J. Fairhurst, *Law of the European Community* (4th ed., Pearson, 2003)

CASEBOOKS

F. Emmert, *European Union Law—Cases* (Kluwer Law International, 2000)

B. Rudden, and D.R. Phelan, *Basic Community Cases* (2nd ed., OUP, 1997)

STUDY SKILL TECHNIQUES

K. Fullerton and M. Macgregor, *Legal Research Skills for Scots Lawyers* (W. Green & Sons, 1999)

P. Clinch, *Using a Law Library* (Blackstone Press, 2001)
S. Stein, *Law on the Web—a Guide for Students and Practitioners* (Pearson 2003)
S. I. Strong, *How to Write Law Essays and Exams* (LexisNexis 2003)

LEGISLATION—TREATIES, MAIN REGULATIONS AND DIRECTIVES, ETC.

Rudden and Wyatt, *Basic Community Laws* (7th ed., OUP, 1999)
N. Foster, *Blackstones EC Legislation 2003/04*
Sweet & Maxwell's EU Law Statutes 2003/04

JUDGMENTS OF THE EUROPEAN COURT OF JUSTICE AND THE COURT OF FIRST INSTANCE

These are reproduced in the European Court Reports (E.C.R.) and the Common Market Law Reports (C.M.L.R.).

JOURNALS

European Law Review—E.L.Rev.
Common Market Law Review—C.M.L.Rev.
European Public Law—E.P.L.
Journal of Common Market Studies—J.C.M.S.
European Competition Law Review—E.C.L.R.

INTERNET

One of the most important sources of information is the web site of the European Union (the Europa Server)—http://europa.eu.int

This site is the gateway to all policies, legislation and institutions of the EU It gives multilingual access to all major issues on the EU agenda: Treaties and legislation, the Official Journal, information on the rights of European citizens, press releases from the institutions, information on the euro (€), up-to-date information on decisions, programmes or measures adopted by the EU, publications and statistics, the nearest available sources of information and caselaw from the European Courts of Justice.

What's New on Europa
http://europa.eu.int/geninfo/whatsnew/htm
RAPID: EU Press Releases
http://europa.eu.int/en/comm/spp/rapid.html
EUR-Lex, access to a mass of full-text legislative information including Treaties, legislative measures, case law and the Official Journal
http://europa.eu.int/eur-lex/en/index.html
European Parliament
http://www.europarl.eu.int/home/default_en.htm
Council of the EU
http://ue.eu.int/en/summ.htm
European Commission
http://europa.eu.int/comm/index_en.htm

Court of Justice
                              http://curia.eu.int/en/index.htm
Court of Auditors
                         http://www.eca.eu.int/EN/menu.htm
Committee of the Regions
                                     http://www.cor.eu.int/

KEEPING UP TO DATE

BBC World Service: Europe Today
                    http://www.bbc.co.uk/worldservice/europetoday

Yahoo: News Headlines: European Union
        http://search.news.yahoo.com/search/news/?p=%22European+Union

---

4. SOURCES OF LAW

The founding Treaties do not define the sources of Community law. Article 220 (ex Article 164) simply states that "The Court of Justice shall ensure that in the interpretation and application of this Treaty the law is observed". However, reflecting the diversity and supranational nature of the Community legal system, the sources of law can be classified into the following four main sources.

(1) TREATIES

The three Community Treaties which are the primary source of Community law and its ultimate legal authority:

- European Coal and Steel Community Treaty 1951 (expires 2002);
- European Economic Community Treaty 1957 (now the EC Treaty); and
- Euratom Treaty 1957.

Other Treaties made between Member States including those amending the founding treaties and accession treaties of new Member States:

- Merger Treaty 1965;
- Budgetary Treaties 1970; 1975;
- Single European Act 1986;
- Treaty on European Union 1992 (the Maastricht Treaty);
- Treaty of Amsterdam 1997;
- Treaty of Nice 2000; and
- Treaties of accession of Denmark, Ireland and the UK in 1972, Greece in 1981, Spain and Portugal in 1986, and Austria, Finland and Sweden in 1994, and Cyprus, the Czech Republic, Estonia, Hungary, Latvia, Lithuania, Malta, Poland, Slovakia and Slovenia in 2003.

Treaties between the Communities and non-Member States

- Treaty establishing the World Trade Organisation;
- Lomé Conventions with the African, Caribbean and Pacific (ACP) countries; and
- Europe Agreements between the European Community and applicant countries for membership of the European Union.

(2) SECONDARY LEGISLATION

This refers to the body of Community rules adopted in accordance with the founding Treaties. It has evolved over the years from the 100 Articles of the ECSC Treaty, into a vast body of law comprising thousands of Regulations, Directives, Decisions, Agreements and other measures. These are the binding and non-binding Acts of the Institutions. Each institution must act within the limits of the powers conferred upon it by Article 249 (ex Article 189) which states:

> "In order to carry out their task and in accordance with the provisions of this Treaty, the European Parliament acting jointly with the Council, the Council and the Commission shall make regulations and issue directives, take decisions, make recommendations or deliver opinions.
> A regulation shall have general application. It shall be binding in its entirety and directly applicable in all Member States.
> A directive shall be binding, as to the result to be achieved, upon each Member State to which it is addressed, but shall leave to the national authorities the choice of form and methods.
> A decision shall be binding in its entirety upon those to whom it is addressed.
> Recommendations and opinions shall have no binding force."

Article 249 therefore sets out three types of legally binding acts

- Regulations
- Directives
- Decisions

And two types of non-legally binding acts

- Recommendations
- Opinions

Legislation Must Have a Legal Basis

Whichever form of legislation is chosen, it fulfils a specific function in the development of Community law and therefore the Treaty specifies which type of act must be adopted to achieve a particular aim of the Community. The preamble to any piece of legislation should therefore state the Article of the Treaty on which it is based. The Treaty Article chosen will set out the legislative procedure to be followed—involving voting requirements in the Council and the extent of the European Parliament's involvement in the process.

Article 253 (ex Article 190) sets out that Regulations, Directives and Decisions all must state the reasons on which they are based and must refer to the proposals and opinions which were required by the Treaty to be obtained. The institution concerned is not allowed to specify how it would *prefer* the objective to be pursued. Its conviction must be based on objective factors, which must be amenable to judicial review. In particular, these factors must include the aim and content of the measure (*Commission v Council Re Titanium Dioxide Waste* [1991]). The measure must therefore specify in a clear and concise manner what the principal issues of fact and law so that the reasoning which led the institution to make its choice of legal basis may be clearly understood. If an act of an institution is not sufficiently reasoned, this constitutes a ground for annulment of the measure (see Chapter 7, Judicial Review).

The full citation convention for secondary legislation is as follows:

- Form of legislation (Regulation, Directive, etc.);
- Number of the instrument and its year of adoption (Regulations are cited by number then year, Directives and Decisions by year then number);
- Treaty from which authority for the legislation is founded;
- The institution adopting the legislation (Commission, Council);
- Date passed;
- Title; and
- Date and page number of the Official Journal in which the measure was published.

For example—Directive 2001/37/EC of the European Parliament and of the Council of 5 June 2001 on the approximation of the laws, regulations and administrative provisions of the Member States concerning the manufacture, presentation and sale of tobacco products ([2001] O.J. L194/26).

Regulations

"A regulation shall have general application. It shall be binding in its entirety and directly applicable in all Member States".

- "General application" means that a Regulation applies to any number of Member States, individuals or companies;
- "Binding in its entirety" means that the whole of the Regulation must be implemented;
- "Directly applicable" means that the Regulation applies in all Member States without the need for further enactment;
- "in all Member States" means that the Regulation must be applied in the same way and at the same time in all Member States; and
- Regulations must be published in the Official Journal in the eleven official Community languages. They enter into force on the date specified in the act, or if no date is specified, then on the twentieth day following their publication.

Directives

"A directive shall be binding, as to the result to be achieved, upon each Member State to which it is addressed, but shall leave it to the national authorities the choice of form and methods."

- The purpose of Directives is to allow the achievement of common objectives throughout the Member States;
- Directives are addressed to Member States only;
- The Member State must enact domestic legislation to comply with the Directive within a set time limit;
- The form of the implementing legislation is chosen by the Member State which can choose the most appropriate method for its own legal system;
- Once they have been correctly transposed into national law, Directives are binding on individuals;
- Individuals may claim compensation if a Member State fails to implement a Directive within the time limit or does so incompletely or incorrectly; and
- Directives must be published in the Official Journal in the eleven official Community languages.

Decisions

"A decision shall be binding in its entirely upon those to whom it is addressed."

- "Binding in its entirety" means that the whole of the Decision must be implemented;
- A Decision is binding only upon those to whom it is addressed;
- A Decision can be addressed to a Member State or to an individual or company;
- There is no need to enact implementing legislation;
- Decisions must be notified to those to whom they are addressed and do not come into effect until that notification has been carried out;
- Decisions can be challenged before the Court of Justice by persons who claim to be directly and individually affected; and
- Decisions affecting the rights of third parties are published in the Official Journal in the eleven official Community languages.

Recommendations and Opinions

"Recommendations and opinions shall have no binding force". They are of persuasive force only.

(3) CASELAW OF THE EUROPEAN COURT OF JUSTICE AND THE COURT OF FIRST INSTANCE

The decisions of the Court of Justice are authoritative on all aspects of the Treaties, acts of the Institutions and acts of the Member States which arise in conformity with their Treaty obligations. Unlike the common law tradition of Anglo-American systems, the civilian nature of Community law based on Continental legal systems does not rely on the doctrine of precedent and means that the Court of Justice is not rigidly bound by its own previous decisions. It may therefore depart from them if it feels the need to adapt or update its caselaw (*Keck and Mithouard* [1993]).

(4) GENERAL PRINCIPLES OF LAW

As well as the Treaties, the Court of Justice draws on general principles of law derived from the legal traditions of the Member States. These general principles can be used by all courts to interpret Community law. They are generally recognised as comprising:

- Proportionality—legislative measures should not go beyond what is necessary to achieve the desired objective (*Bela-Mühle v Grows Farm* [1977]);
- Legal certainty—comprising respect for legitimate expectations and the principle that European Community measures should not have retroactive effect (*Council v European Parliament* [1986]);
- Legitimate expectation (*Mulder v Minister van Landbouw en Visserij* [1988]);
- Legal Professional Privilege—written communication between independent (not in-house) lawyers and clients are respected (*A M & S Europe Limited v Commission* [1982]); and
- Fundamental Human Rights—in *Nold v Commission* [1974] the Court stated that while it was inspired by the constitutional traditions common to the Member States, it added "international treaties for the protection of human rights" which was clearly a reference to the European Convention for the Protection of Human Rights and Fundamental Freedoms.

---

5. INSTITUTIONS

Although the three European Communities (ECSC, Euratom and EEC) were originally endowed with their own separate institutions, modifications over the years meant that by the early 1990s a single institutional framework was in place, serving all three Communities. The nature of these institutions is unique not only in their structure but in the way they interact in the performance of the legislative, executive and judicial functions of the Community.

There are four main institutions:

- European Commission (formerly known as the High Authority) which acts in the interests of the Community;
- Council of the European Union (formerly known as the Council of Ministers) representing the Member States;
- European Parliament (formerly known as the Assembly) representing the peoples of Europe; and
- Court of Justice (to which in 1986 was added a Court of First Instance).

The Treaty on European Union signed in 1992 created a fifth institution:

• Court of Auditors

What distinguishes an institution from any other Community body is that an institution may take binding decisions and that their members are either elected nationally (as in the case of the Council and the European Parliament) or appointed by the governments of the Member States or by the Council. Other bodies such as the Committee of the Regions either play a purely consultative role or take decisions which are not binding.

The supreme political authority of the Community, formulating and directing policy initiatives is

• The European Council

Three other bodies have been created, although they do not hold the status of "institutions". These are:

• Economic and Social Committee—an advisory committee comprised of no more than 350 representatives of various economic and social groups such as "producers, farmers, carriers, workers, dealers, craftsmen, professional occupations, consumers and the general public". (Articles 257 to 262);
• Committee of the Regions—a consultative committee limited to 350 members of local and regional authorities holding an electoral mandate to represent citizens at a local level. The Committee advises on matters of particular concern to European regions. In particular, the Treaty provides for it to be consulted in the areas of culture, public health, economic and social cohesion and environmental policy (Articles 263 and 264); and
• European Investment Bank—set up to manage the Structural Fund and other Community funds on a non-profit-making basis to aid the less developed regions and to assist in funding projects affecting more than one Member State where they cannot be funded sufficiently from within those Member States themselves (Articles 266 and 267).

THE EUROPEAN COMMISSION

Composition
The Commission is composed of 20 Commissioners, two for the major countries (Germany, France, Italy, Spain and the UK) and one for each of the other countries. From January 2005, with an enlarged European Union of 25 Member States, the Commission will include one national of each Member State, reducing the five larger Member States' representation from two to one. Further provision concerning the size of the Commission was set out in the Treaty of Nice to the effect that if and when the Union consists of 27 Member States, the Commissioners will number less than the Member States, the exact number and nationality to be agreed by the Council of Ministers acting unanimously and based on the principles of equality, demography and geography.

The method by which the Commission will be appointed is that after consulting the European Parliament, the Member States first nominate the

President of the Commission by qualified majority. Thereafter, in consultation with the President they nominate individual Commissioners for a renewable five-year term who are chosen on grounds of their general competence and "whose independence is beyond doubt". The Commission as a body is then subject to a vote of approval by the European Parliament. The Parliament may not choose which of the Commissioners it likes (or dislikes). Approval is by a vote of confidence en bloc. After approval by the Parliament, they are appointed by the governments of the respective Member States.

The Commission is subject to other supervision by the Parliament which:

*   May censure the Commission;
*   Must receive monthly reports from the Commission on the implementation of the budget; and
*   Must be presented with the Commission's Annual General Report.

To ensure their independence Commissioners are forbidden to seek or take instructions from any government or other body and must refrain from any action which is not compatible with their duties. All the Member States have accepted this principle and no influence is brought to bear upon the Commissioners in the performance of their tasks. Their duties are solely to further the wider interests of the Community. During their term of office, Commissioners may not engage in any other occupation and even after they retire, they are bound to behave with integrity and discretion as regards the acceptance of certain appointments or benefits.

A Commissioner will be forced to resign if the President requests such resignation, having first of all obtained the collective approval of the Commission.

As well as allowing Commissioners to fulfil their tasks with complete impartiality, the collegiate nature of the Commission also protects them from undue pressure. Commissioners do not fulfil individual roles under the Treaty. Decisions are thus made by simple majority, dissenting opinions are not published and all members of the college of Commissioners bear collective responsibility on the political level for all decisions adopted.

Functions and Powers
The administrative responsibility of the Commission is divided up into 23 Directorates-General, at least one of which is allocated by the President to the portfolio of an individual Commissioner. They cover such specific areas of responsibility such as External Relations (DGI), competition (DGIV), and so on. Each Commissioner is assisted by a Cabinet headed by a Chef de Cabinet. There are also specialised services such as the Legal Service which advises the Directorates-General and represent the Commission in legal proceedings, and the Statistical and Publications Office. The total staff of the Commission is approximately 19,000, of whom about 4,000 are interpreters.

The Commission's powers and functions are laid down in the Treaty under Article 211 (ex Article 155) to Article 219 (ex Article 163). They fall into three main categories.

(1) Guardian of the Treaties

The Commission has been given the power to ensure that the provisions of the Treaty and the measures adopted for their implementation are applied.

It monitors the performance of the Member States in complying with their Treaty obligations and may receive complaints from individuals or companies who believe that a Member State is infringing their Community rights. Under Article 226 (ex Article 169) proceedings the Commission may investigate and prosecute Member States alleged to be in breach of their Treaty obligations.

These obligations (sometimes known as "the loyalty clause" of the Treaty) are set out in Article 10 (ex Article 5) which states that:

> "Member States must take all appropriate measures, whether general or particular, to ensure fulfilment of the obligations arising out of this Treaty or resulting from action taken by the institutions of the Community. They shall facilitate the achievement of the Community's tasks. They shall abstain from any measure which could jeopardise the attainment of the objectives of this Treaty".

When the Commission considers that a Member State has not fulfilled an obligation under Community law, it takes the following steps:

* It reminds the government in question of its obligations and invites it to take the necessary measures or submit its observations, all within a time limit set by the Commission, normally two months;
* If no action is taken by the Member State and no observations are received, or if those that were submitted do not convince the Commission, it delivers a "reasoned opinion" on the matter and lays down a time limit within which the Member State must comply;
* If the Member State does not comply, the Commission may bring the matter before the Court of Justice; and
* If the Court finds that the Member State has indeed failed to fulfil its obligation, "the State shall be required to take the necessary steps to comply with the judgment".

The procedure for enforcing Member States' fulfilment of their Community obligations is therefore in two stages. The first is an informal stage during which the Commission issues the formal notice and eventually a reasoned opinion to the Member State. In practice though, the Commission endeavours to negotiate a settlement. The second stage is the formal judicial stage where the Commission refers the Member State to the Court of Justice.

There is also a right for a Member State to take action against another Member State under Article 227 for failure to fulfil its Community obligations. The procedure requires that the matter be brought to the attention of the Commission. Proceedings then mirror those under Article 226, with the added requirement that the Commission requests the observations of *both* Member States involved. Actions brought under this heading are extremely rare as this procedure tends to be politically contentious. To date, only two cases have reached the Court, *France v UK* [1979] and *Belgium v Spain* [2000].

Since 1993, Article 228(2) (ex Article 171(2)) of the Treaty now provides that in cases where the Member State has not taken the necessary steps to comply with the judgment of the Court, it shall, after giving the Member State the opportunity to submit its observations, issue a reasoned opinion specifying the points on which the Member State has not complied and fixing a time limit for this to be carried out. In case of non-compliance, the Commission may bring the matter again to the Court and specify the amount of the lump sum or penalty payment to be paid. If the Court finds that the Member State has indeed not complied with its judgment, it may impose a lump sum or penalty payment (*Commission v Greece [2000]*). As well as the penalties provided for in the Treaty to encourage Member States to fulfil their Community obligations, pecuniary sanctions can also be imposed on Member States where they breach Community law to the detriment of an individual (see Member State Liability, p.36).

The Commission also monitors the acts of the Council, the Parliament and the European Central Bank and may initiate an action against them when it is believed that:

- Their failure to act constitutes an infringement of the Treaty (Article 232 ex Article 175); **or**
- An act of the institution constitutes an infringement of the Treaty (Article 230 ex Article 173).

(2) Initiator of Community Action

The Commission has historically had the right of legislative initiative in that it is empowered to propose legislation for its adoption by the Council and the European Parliament acting in accordance with the Community's legislative procedures. Legislation must encompass three core objectives. First, the Commission must identify the European interest; secondly, it must organise consultation as widely as necessary and thirdly, it must respect the principle of subsidiarity (*see* Chapter 6, European Law and National Law). In fulfilment of this task the Commission works closely with the Union's two consultative bodies, the Economic and Social Committee and the Committee of the Regions, and consults them on most items of draft legislation.

The Treaty on European Union now allows the Council and Parliament to request that the Commission submits appropriate proposals for legislation where these are required for the purpose of implementing the Treaty.

The Commission will then issue preparatory documents such as Green Papers containing a description of a problem and its proposal for solving it; this will be followed by a White Paper outlining the proposed legislation for consultation. The general principle of transparency that the public should have the widest possible access to documents held by the Commission, the Parliament and the Council—subject to public interest or the rights of privacy of the individual—has been adopted through Regulation 1049/2001 which sets out that refusal to grant access must be based on one of the exceptions provided for within the Regulation and must be justified on the grounds that disclosure of the document in question would be harmful.

The Commission's significant role in shaping the Community's priorities has increased in importance over recent years—for example in preparing for the completion of the single market and for enlargement of the Union in the twenty-first century. In July 2001 the Commission also initiated a wide-ranging debate throughout the Member States by publishing a major White Paper on the Reform of European Governance, paving the way for the Convention on the Future of Europe.

(3) Executive of the Community

The Commission has been given its own power of decision which it exercises in the functioning and development of the common market, for example in furtherance of the Community's competition policy where it administers and enforces the competition rules, and regulates mergers, joint ventures and acquisitions.

It also administers the customs union, the common agricultural policy, state aids and the common commercial policy. Although the majority of European policies are administered by the Member States themselves the Commission has significant supervisory powers. In this connection it may make regulations which must be observed within the Member States and ensures that these regulations are carried out.

A significant part of its executive function is to manage the Community budget for submission to the Council and administer special funds such as the European Agricultural Guidance and Guarantee Fund, the European Regional Development Fund, the Cohesion Fund and the European Social Fund which form part of the budget.

Under the Euratom Treaty, the Commission has also been given the power to borrow on the world financial markets and to loan money for the financing of atomic energy projects. It also finances infrastructure and industrial projects. The borrowing is carried out by the Commission but the administration of the resources thus acquired is carried out by the European Investment Bank.

The Commission also acts as negotiator of international trade and co-operation agreements with third countries, or groups of countries, which the Council then concludes.

The Commission can also act by way of delegated legislative power from the Council, known as "Comitology". This practice of decision-making involves the Commission's legislative activities being supervised by the Council under a complex system involving the submission of the Commission's draft implementing measures to committees composed of officials from Member States.

The European institutional structure is not characterised by a rigid separation of powers. The Commission for example plays a role that is by turns legislative, executive, judicial and administrative. It is:

- The guardian of the Treaties;
- Initiator and co-ordinator of Community policy; and
- The executive agency of the Community.

COUNCIL OF THE EUROPEAN UNION ("THE COUNCIL")

The Council—also referred to as the Council of Ministers—is a body with the characteristics of both a supranational and an intergovernmental organisation. That is to say, it acts as a major player in Community decision-making and has a substantial role to play under the other two "pillars" of the European Union involving co-operation between the Union's Member States. It is composed of representatives from the Member States at ministerial level, authorised to commit the government of that Member State. In practice this means that its membership fluctuates depending on the subject under discussion. For example, the General Affairs Council deals with institutional and policy issues and is attended by national Foreign Ministers. Ministers for Agriculture, Transport, Finance, etc., constitute the membership of the Council when it discusses policy and legislation in those areas.

The Council is assisted in its work by COREPER (The Committee of Permanent Representatives) consisting of senior national ambassadors and their deputies who are permanently located in Brussels. The work of this Committee allows decisions to be made by the Council by examining Commission proposals and preparing items for discussion at Council meetings. COREPER is assisted by a range of specialist advisory committees.

(1) Under the European Community Treaty, the Council's powers and functions are laid down in the under Article 202 (ex Article 145) to Article 210 (ex Article 154). The Council:

- Is the European Union's main decision-making institution and final legislative authority exercising power for the whole spectrum of the Community's activities.

    The Treaty on European Union strengthened the role of the European Parliament and now many of the Council's powers must be shared with Parliament. These relate not only to budgetary power (where it has always been the case), but also to the introduction of a co-decision procedure for enacting legislation. As a consequence, a wide range of legislation such as that relating to the single market, consumer affairs, trans-European networks, education and health is adopted jointly by both the Parliament and the Council.

    Depending on the subject under discussion and the voting procedures specified in the Treaty, the Council acts by a simple majority of its members, by a qualified majority or by unanimous decision. Where the Council acts by a qualified majority, the votes of each of its members are weighted as follows:

Country	Number of Votes	After January 1, 2005
Austria	4	10
Belgium	5	12
Denmark	3	7
Finland	3	7
France	10	29
Germany	10	29
Greece	5	12
Ireland	3	7

Italy	10	29
Luxembourg	2	4
Netherlands	5	13
Portugal	5	12
Spain	8	27
Sweden	4	10
United Kingdom	10	29
Cyprus		4
Czech Republic		12
Estonia		4
Hungary		12
Latvia		4
Lithuania		7
Malta		3
Poland		27
Slovakia		7
Slovenia		4
Bulgaria		10
Romania		14

For example, if the Commission considers that a proposal on certain aspects of tackling unemployment throughout the Community is required, it may table a proposal under Title VIII (Employment) of the Treaty. Within that title, Article 129 (ex Article 109r) sets out:

"The Council, acting in accordance with the procedure referred to in Article 251 and after consulting the Economic and Social Committee and the Committee of the Regions, may adopt incentive measures designed to encourage co-operation between Member States and to support their action in the field of employment through initiatives aimed at developing exchanges of information and best practices".

This means that Article 251 which sets out the co-decision procedure in detail, must be used. In turn Article 251 specifies the voting procedure necessary within the Council in order to enact the legislation proposed by the Commission. In this case it is qualified majority voting.

For matters within the Community "pillar" most of the decisions are taken by qualified majority. There are some areas of Community action, however which still remain subject to unanimity. These include taxation, industry, culture, regional and social funds and the framework programme for research and technology development.

Since the Treaty of Nice, acts of the Council will require at least 170 votes in favour, which must be cast by at least a majority of the Member States. This 170-vote threshold will be amended as new Member States are admitted to the Union, with 258 votes required to adopt a measure once the Union reaches 27 members. Additionally, a new provision to take into account the population of the Member States, provides that when a decision is to be adopted by the Council acting by qualified majority, a Member State can request verification that the qualified majority comprises at least 62 per cent of the total population of the Union before the act may be adopted.

Legislation takes the form of Regulations, Directives, Decisions, Recommendations and Opinions (*see* Chapter 4, Sources of Law).

The Council may also adopt conclusions of a political nature or other types of acts such as Declarations or Resolutions. Furthermore, the Council establishes requirements for the Commission to exercise the implementing powers conferred upon it.

Until recently, voting in the Council remained secret. The Treaty of Amsterdam however has provided for more transparency by allowing greater access to Council, Commission and European Parliament documents, subject to limits on the grounds of public and private interest. (*see* above, under "The Commission").

Community legislation as well as the Council's common positions forwarded to the European Parliament are published in the Official Journal in all eleven official languages.

The Council also:

- Is the co-ordinator of the general economic policies of the Member States (subject to the principle of subsidiarity);
- Concludes international agreements on behalf of the European Communities (which are negotiated by the Commission and require, in some cases, Parliament's consultation or assent) between the Communities and a State, a group of States or international organisations; and
- Together with the European Parliament, adopts the Community budget after its preparation by the Commission.

(2) Under the Treaty on European Union and by unanimous vote—except for joint actions where qualified majority voting is the rule—the Council:

- Takes the decisions necessary to define and implement the Common Foreign and Security Policy by deciding on joint actions and common positions; and
- Co-ordinates the activities of the Member States, decides on common positions and framework decisions, draws up conventions and adopts measures under the third "pillar" of the European Union, Police and Judicial Co-operation in Criminal Matters.

The Presidency of the Council is held by each Member State on a six-monthly rotating basis and plays a vital part as the driving force in the legislative and political decision-making process. It organises and chairs all meetings and works out compromises to resolve difficulties. The Presidency, assisted by the Secretary-General of the Council who also acts as High Representative for the Common Foreign and Security Policy, also represents the Union for foreign and security matters.

THE EUROPEAN PARLIAMENT

Composition

The European Parliament presently consists of 626 members representing 375 million citizens in 15 Member States of the European Union and since 1979 has been directly elected every five years throughout all the Member States. The Treaty of Nice provides for the number of MEPs not to exceed 732. From June 2004, the Parliament will include members from the ten countries joining the Union in May 2004. Citizens of the European Union as well as citizens of the Union living in a Member State of which they are not nationals, are eligible to vote and stand for election.

With effect from the new Parliament elected in June 2004, the allocation of seats will be: 99 for Germany, 72 for France, Italy and the UK, 50 for Spain, 25 for the Netherlands, 22 for Belgium, Greece and Portugal, 18 for Sweden, 17 for Austria, 13 for Denmark and Finland, 12 for Ireland and 6 for Luxembourg. The new Member States' allocation of seats will be 5 for Malta, 6 for Cyprus and Estonia, 7 for Slovenia, 8 for Hungary, 12 for Lithuania, 13 for Slovakia, 20 for the Czech Republic and 50 for Poland.

MEPs sit in political groups rather than in national delegations. Though its committee meetings generally take place in Brussels, it meets in plenary sitting at Strasbourg for one week a month. Parliament's secretariat is located in Luxembourg. During its sessions, simultaneous translation of its debates is provided and all documentation is translated and published in the Official Journal in the official Community languages. It elects its own President and 14 Vice-Presidents who together form "the Bureau"—the executive body which drafts agendas, decides on matters of competence and makes the preliminary draft of Parliament's budget.

As well as exercising its three main functions (below) Parliament takes an active part in Europe's political life by commissioning reports and passing resolutions on issues of a social and political nature such as concern for human rights. It has also contributed in no small measure to the establishment of a European Veterinary Agency in Dublin and the creation of the European Anti-Fraud Office for budgetary matters.

Functions and Powers

The functions and powers of Parliament are laid out in Articles 189 (ex Article 137) to Article 201 (ex Article 144). They fall into three main categories:

- Supervisory
- Legislative
- Budgetary

Supervisory

Parliament has general supervisory powers over the other institutions of which the most powerful is its ability to hold the Commission accountable for its activities.

At the request of a quarter of its members, Parliament may set up temporary Committees of Inquiry to investigate alleged contraventions or maladministration in the implementation of European law, and to appoint a

Parliamentary Ombudsman to investigate complaints such as discrimination, refusal of information or needless delays on the part of other institutions (except for the Court of Justice and the Court of First Instance).

It may receive petitions from individuals or companies in the Member States on any matter within the Union's fields of activities.

Members of the European Parliament can put written or oral questions to the Commission and to the Council or make recommendations.

Legislative
Originally, the Treaty of Rome allowed the European Parliament to act only in a consultative capacity. The Treaty on European Union and the Treaty of Amsterdam have extended this purely advisory role to one which fully involves Parliament in the legislative process. In many areas the power of decision is now shared by the Council and Parliament. The extent to which this is exercised is specified within the Treaty depending on the nature of the provision authorising action by the Community for a particular purpose (the legal basis).

Normally legislation is enacted by one of the three main procedures—co-decision, consultation or assent. There is also a fourth procedure—the co-operation procedure—allowing Parliament two readings of proposals but containing no provision for compulsory conciliation. The Treaties of Amsterdam and Nice significantly extended the scope of the co-decision procedure which means that in practice it has almost entirely replaced the co-operation procedure.

(a) Co-decision procedure
This procedure is laid down in Article 251 (ex Article 189b) and enables Parliament to share decision-making power equally with the Council. A legal act is adopted if Council and Parliament agree at first reading. If they disagree, a "conciliation committee" composed of equal numbers of MEPs and members of the Council, with the Commission present, endeavours to find a compromise on which both the Council and Parliament can subsequently agree. However, if agreement does not result Parliament can reject the proposal outright by an absolute majority. The co-decision procedure applies to a range of issues such as the free movement of workers, consumer protection, education, culture, health and trans-European networks.

(b) Consultation procedure
The consultation procedure requires an opinion from Parliament before the Council can adopt a legislative proposal from the Commission. Neither the Commission nor the Council is obliged to accept Parliament's amendments. Once Parliament has given its opinion, the Council can adopt the proposal without amendments or adopt it in an amended form. The consultation procedure applies to the common agricultural policy, harmonisation of indirect taxation, aspects of environmental policy and matters connected with Economic and Monetary Union.

(c) Assent procedure
The assent procedure applies to those legislative areas in which the Council acts by unanimous decision. Since the Treaty of Amsterdam this has been limited to the organisation and objectives of the Structural and Cohesion

Funds. Parliament's assent is also required for international agreements concluded between the Union and a non-member country or group of countries, such as the accession of new Member States and association agreements with third countries (absolute majority of Parliament's total membership required).

Budgetary

The European Parliament is jointly involved with the Council in the budgetary procedure from the preparation stage, notably in laying down the general guidelines and the type of spending, voting on the annual budget prepared by the Commission and overseeing its implementation (Article 272 ex Article 203).

Its main power concerns the non-compulsory items on the budget such as social and regional policy, research and aid to Central and Eastern non-member countries. The compulsory items of the Community's budget—mainly those relating to the Common Agricultural Policy—call for a more limited input from Parliament.

THE COURTS OF JUSTICE OF THE EUROPEAN COMMUNITIES

The origins of the Court of Justice can be traced to the founding Treaties (ECSC, Euratom and the EEC) which established a Court of Justice for each Community. These have since been merged into one single Court of Justice for the European Communities. Although the Treaty refers to it as "the Court of Justice" it is also known as the European Court of Justice or the European Court. Both Community Courts (the Court of Justice and its associated Court of First Instance) are based in Luxembourg. They should not be confused with the European Court of Human Rights which has its home in Strasbourg which is *not* an institution of the European Union. It is the role of the Court of Justice to be the guardian of European Community law in accordance with Article 220 (ex Article 164) which states simply that "The Court of Justice shall ensure that in the interpretation and application of this Treaty the law is observed". The law referred to consists of the Treaties, secondary legislation (such as Regulations, Directives and Decisions) and the case-law of the Court itself. The Court of First Instance operates under Article 225 (ex Article 168a).

The Court of Justice

Composition

From May 2004, the Court will consist of 25 judges, one from each Member State. It sits in plenary session when a Member State or a Community institution which is party to the proceedings so requests, or when the Court itself decides. In all other cases it sits in chambers of three or five Judges. A new Grand Chamber consisting of 11 Judges will sit whenever a Member State or Community institution that is a party to the proceedings requests. In addition, if it is considered that a case before it is of exceptional importance, the Court, after consultation with the Advocate-General in the matter, may decide to refer the case to the plenary session. Its deliberations take place in private and result in a single, collegiate judgment. The working language of the Court is French, though documents are translated into all official languages of the Community.

The Court is assisted by eight Advocates-General whose task it is to examine the cases and deliver reasoned opinions to the Court. Both Judges and Advocates-General are appointed for a period of six years. The President of the Court is elected every three years by its Judges, who are chosen from those

> "whose independence is beyond doubt and who possess the qualifications required for appointment to the highest judicial offices in their respective countries or who are jurisconsults of recognised competence by common accord of the governments of the Member States."

Each Member State has a judge on the Court to represent the legal tradition of that particular country rather than the Member State itself. The Court is also assisted by a Registrar, Legal Secretaries and two Directorates.

Functions and Powers

The Court's functions and powers are set out in Article 220 (ex Article 164) to Article 245 (ex Article 188) as well as within its own Rules of Procedure ([1991] O.J. L176/7).

The Court has four main areas of jurisdiction. It may rule on

(1) Infringement actions against Member States, particularly
(a) Commission v Member States (Article 226 ex Article 169)
(b) Member State v Member State (Article 227 ex Article 170)
(c) Member State's failure to fulfil a Treaty obligation (Article 228 ex Article 171).

(2) Non-contractual liability of the Community (Article 288 ex Article 215) and Compensation for damage in that event (Article 235 ex Article 178).

(3) The legality of Community action or inaction (Article 230 ex Article 173 and Article 232 ex Article 175).

(4) Preliminary rulings on the interpretation and validity of European law at the request of a national court or tribunal (Article 234 ex Article 177).

In order to enforce a judgment, the Commission may bring a further infringement action against a Member State under Article 228 (ex Article 171). Since 1993, the Court has also been given the power to impose a financial penalty on a Member State if that state still refuses to comply with the Court's judgment or its Treaty obligations (Article 228(2) ex Article 171(2)).

The Court also has jurisdiction to rule on:

• Disputes concerning the European Investment Bank (Article 237 ex Article 180);
• On arbitration clauses contained in a contract concluded by or on behalf of the Community (Article 238 ex Article 181);

- Disputes submitted under special agreements (Article 239 ex Article 182); and
- Compatibility with the Treaties of international agreements entered into by the Community (Article 300(6) ex Article 228(6)).

The Court of Justice acts both as a court of first instance and as an appeal court from the Court of First Instance.

Its procedure generally falls into four stages (though the second stage is often omitted):

- Written proceedings;
- Investigation or preparatory inquiry;
- Oral proceedings; and
- Judgment (the formal ruling of which is published in the Official Journal and the full judgment together with the Advocate-General's opinion, in the European Court Reports (E.C.R.) in all Community languages.

The Court of First Instance
To ease the workload of the Court of Justice, the Single European Act provided for the creation of a new Court of First Instance. It began sitting in 1989, with limited jurisdiction—staff cases, competition and anti-dumping cases and some matters relation to the ECSC and Euratom. Since 1993 it has heard all cases brought by natural or legal persons including actions for judicial review and actions for damages against Community institutions or the Member States. Since February 2003, the structure, functions and rules of the Court of First Instance have been substantially reformed due to the delays because of workload coupled with the imminent enlargement of the Union to 25 Member States in May 2004. Changes have included:

- Judicial panels with a right of appeal on points of law to the CFI.
- Jurisdiction to hear and determine at first instance actions on Judicial Review, Failure to Act, non-contractual liability of the Community, staff disputes and disputes concerning the European Investment Bank and national central banks (with the exception of those reserved in the Court's Statute for hearing before the Court of Justice). There is a right of appeal to the Court of Justice on points of law only.
- Increased jurisdiction particularly with regard to the right to examine questions previously referred only to the Court of Justice for interpretation (*see* Chapter 8, Preliminary Rulings) in specified areas and under certain conditions.
- If there is a serious risk of the unity or consistency of Community law being affected, the Court of First Instance's first Advocate-General may propose, within one month of the CFI's decision, that the Court of Justice reviews the decision of the CFI.
- The Court of First Instance may sit in chambers of three or five judges, with provisions for plenary session, a single judge and the establishment of a Grand Chamber of 11 Judges.

The Court of First Instance consists of at least one Judge from each Member State appointed under the same criteria as the Judges of the Court of Justice.

COURT OF AUDITORS

The Court of Auditors was set up in 1975 to control and supervise the implementation of the budget. It became a full institution in 1993 under the Treaty on European Union. Its main function is to scrutinise the Commission's management of the Community budget, examine its legality, regularity of revenue and expenditure and ensure its sound financial management. As an independent audit body (rather than a "court"), it is also viewed by Parliament as an essential tool in establishing greater financial control and good management of the Community. On the basis of the Court of Auditors' reports, it is the European Parliament which gives the Commission final discharge for the adoption of the annual budget. It is composed of one full-time member chosen by the Council (after consulting the European Parliament) from each Member State among persons who have had relevant auditing experience and whose independence is beyond doubt.

Its powers and functions are set out in Articles 246 (ex Article 188a) to 248 (ex Article 188c).

THE EUROPEAN COUNCIL

As well as these institutions there is also a supreme, policy-making body known as the European Council. It should not be confused with Council of the European Union (above) or with the Council of Europe, an international organisation concerned mainly with human rights and based in Strasbourg.

Since 1974 the informal meetings of Heads of State and Government (previously known as "Summit meetings") have been formalised into twice-yearly meetings hosted by the Member State holding the Presidency of the Union. The President of the Commission also attends these gatherings. Although the European Council possesses no formal powers and thus plays no part in the legislative machinery, its meetings provide momentum for European integration by the injection of political will at the very highest level, to promote co-ordination and clarification of inter-Community relations and set out policy initiatives. It therefore may set out general guidelines for action to be taken at Community level by the Council and the Commission. Its informal discussions also act as a forum for co-ordination of Member States' foreign policies to maximise their influence on world affairs (*See* Article 4 TEU (ex Article D TEU)).

The Treaty of Amsterdam introduced new powers for the European Council allowing it to determine the existence of a "serious and persistent breach by a Member State" of the principles of liberty, democracy, respect for human rights and fundamental freedoms, and the rule of law ... "after inviting the government of the Member State in question to submit its observations." (Article 7 (ex Article F.1 TEU).)

The Presidency of the European Council is held by the Member State holding the six-monthly Presidency of the Council of the European Union.

Accompanied by ever-increasing media attention, the European Council continues to provide a significant focus of authority and leadership for Europe.

6. EUROPEAN LAW AND NATIONAL LAW

DIRECT EFFECT

The three European Communities were set up through an international treaty. International treaties are agreements between states affecting relations between them and do not create rights for citizens. However, the Community legal order differs in that it does create rights within Member States for the nationals of those states, as individuals. Certain provisions of Community law create enforceable private rights for citizens which may be exercised through national courts as if they were part of the law of the land. This individual right is known as "Direct Effect" and means that individuals can pursue their Community rights through their own local courts. Direct effect was not set out in the founding Treaties, but was developed through the caselaw of the Court of Justice.

Direct Effect of Treaty Articles

The leading case is that of *Van Gend en Loos NV v Nederlandse Administratie der Belastingen* [1963]. Van Gend en Loos, a Dutch transport company, imported chemicals from Germany on which it was charged customs duty of eight per cent of the value of the goods. The company challenged this on the grounds that when the EEC Treaty came into effect in the Netherlands, the duty was only three per cent and Article 12 of the Treaty required Member States to refrain from introducing any new customs duties on imports and exports of goods—a negative obligation. The Dutch Customs Authorities argued that the Treaty did not allow an individual the right to bring an action on the grounds of infringement of the Treaty. The Court of Justice disagreed and stated that it was necessary to examine the spirit, general scheme and wording of the provision in question. It stated that the EEC Treaty was more than an international agreement which created obligations between states only. It had established a common market and institutions which had been given powers to legislate not only for its Member States but also for individuals. It continued

> "the Community constitutes a new legal order of international law for the benefit of which the states have limited their sovereign rights, albeit within limited fields and the subjects of which comprise not only Member States but also their nationals. Independently of the legislation of the Member States, Community law therefore not only imposes obligations on individuals but is also intended to confer on them rights which become part of their legal heritage."

The Court then set out the criteria for direct effect to be applicable. For an individual to rely on a provision of European law within a national court, the provision in question:

- Must be clear and unambiguous in its terms;

- Must be unconditional, that is, not subject to any qualifications; and
- Must take effect without any further implementing or discretionary measure either by Member States or by Community institutions.

Van Gend en Loos was soon followed by a number of other similar cases challenging Member States' fulfilment of their Treaty obligations, both negative (refraining from acting in a certain way) and positive (requiring to carry out an action). In such cases, individuals and the state are in a vertical relationship—the state at the apex and the individual beneath, allowing an individual the right to sue a Member State within his own national court when he considers it not to have complied with its Community obligations.

Member State

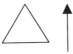

Individuals

Horizontal as well as Vertical Direct Effect?

"Horizontal direct effect" on the other hand, is a relationship between equals—one individual or company—can sue another within a national court to assert rights under European law.

Member State

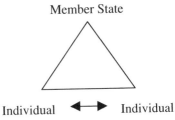

Individual ↔ Individual

In the case of *Defrenne v SABENA* [1976], Ms Defrenne, an air hostess working for the Belgian airline challenged her employer's policy of compulsorily retiring its female cabin crew, but not its male crew, at the age of 40. Ms Defrenne alleged that this was contrary to Article 119 (now Article 141) covering equal pay. Based on the Van Gend en Loos criteria, the Court of Justice stated the provisions of Article 119 produced horizontal direct effect and conferred on Ms Defrenne a right to pursue her Community rights under the Treaty against her employer.

Thus if a Treaty Article satisfies the three criteria set out in the *Van Gend en Loos* case it will produce direct effect—vertical and horizontal—and may be relied upon by individuals. Through the continuing jurisprudence of the Court, Treaty Articles concerning the free movement of goods, persons, equal pay and competition now possess the character of direct effect and allow individuals to pursue their Community rights through their own national courts.

Direct Effect of Regulations
Regulations generally apply directly within Member States without any implementing measures. Article 249 states that "a regulation … shall be … directly applicable in all Member States". Direct applicability however does not necessarily mean that Regulations are directly effective. They still have to satisfy the *Van Gend en Loos* criteria before this is so (*Marimex* [1972]). All that direct applicability means is that there is no need for further legislation to be enacted by Member States incorporating the provision into national law. A Regulation becomes law when it is published in the Official Journal.

Direct Effect of Decisions
Article 249 sets out a decision as being "binding in its entirety upon those to whom it is addressed". In practice a Decision can be addressed to one or more Member States or one or more individuals. If a Decision which is addressed to a Member State fulfils the *Van Gend en Loos* criteria it also can possess direct effect and give rights to individuals (*Grad* [1970]).

Direct Effect of Directives
Directives are never directly applicable. Article 249 states that "a Directive shall be binding as to the result to be achieved" but that the choice of "form and methods" is left to the Member State. Directives thus always require some enacting measure to be carried out and may entail a wide measure of discretion on the part of the Member State. Nevertheless, under certain conditions Directives may be directly effective. In the case of *Grad* as the time limit for implementation had expired, the provisions of the Directive in question requiring Member States to amend their VAT systems could produce direct effect.

In the case of *Van Duyn v Home Office* [1974] the Court examined the wording, nature and general scheme of Directive 64/221 on which Ms Van Duyn relied and stated that a clear and precise obligation had been set out which was not subject to the adoption of subsequent acts on the part either of the Community or of Member States. Finally, the Directive imposed a specific limitation on the discretion of the Member State in the field of public security. Ms Van Duyn's challenge to the Member State (the UK) was allowed by the Court because the effectiveness (*effet utile*) of the Directive would be weakened if individuals were unable to enforce rights conferred on them through the courts. However, it should be noted that direct effect of Directives may be relied upon only:

* After the expiry of the time allowed for its implementation into national law by the Member State (*Ratti* [1978]); and
* If the Member State has incorrectly or incompletely transposed the terms of the Directive into national law (*Emmot* [1990]).

Horizontal as well as Vertical Direct Effect for Directives?
In *Marshall v Southampton Area Health Authority* [1986] the Court had to ascertain whether Directive 79/7 could be relied upon not only against the state but also against another individual or company, as in the *Defrenne* case; in other words, whether Directives could be said to have horizontal as well as vertical direct effect. Miss Marshall had sued her employer whose policy

compelled women to retire at 60, five years earlier than male retirement age. The Court of Justice was asked to rule on whether the Directive had direct effect and if so, whether this could be horizontal as well as vertical. The Court pointed out that Directives are only binding on the Member State to whom they addressed and that therefore "a directive may not of itself, impose obligations on an individual" and "may not be relied upon as such against such a person" but found that Member States had responsibilities towards individuals not simply as public authorities but as employers. It found that the Area Health Authority was an "organ of the state" and that this phrase would cover all organs of the administration including Miss Marshall's employer, as part of the National Health Service. In this case Miss Marshall was able to rely on the Directive as having vertical direct effect.

In a series of subsequent cases, the Court continued to interpret the meaning of "organ of the state" as widely as possible to minimize the inequalities arising when individuals attempted to assert their Community rights against their employers and to prevent a Member State from relying as a defence on its own failure. Difficulties revolved round the question of whether the employer was a public authority (in which case an employee would be allowed to pursue a case based on the vertical direct effect of a Directive) rather than a private business (where the employee would not be able to pursue their Community rights at all). See also:

*   *Foster v British Gas plc* [1990]. This concerned a case brought in pursuance of rights guaranteed by the Equal Treatment Directive 76/207. The Court held that British Gas—a nationalised industry at that time rather than a private company—was an organ of the state as it was offering a public service under the control of a public authority, and was therefore open to challenge through vertical direct effect.
*   *Johnston v Chief Constable of the Royal Ulster Constabulary* [1986]. It was held that a Directive could be relied upon against a Chief Constable as he was responsible to the public for the maintenance of order and safety and was not acting as a private individual.

It was by now quite clear that an individual could pursue rights conferred by an unimplemented Directive against a Member State through the doctrine of vertical direct effect. But inequalities of treatment depending on the status of an employer remained. This was aggravated by Member States sometimes incorporating Directives into national law using precisely the same wording as the original, thus giving them the appearance of Regulations.

In *Faccini Dori v Recreb Srl* [1994] when the Court was asked once again to rule on horizontal direct effect, it resolved the uncertainty once and for all. It emphasised that extending the doctrine of direct effect of Directives to individuals would be "to recognise a power in the Community to enact obligations with immediate effect" a power which previously only related to Regulations. To attribute horizontal direct effect to Directives would therefore establish that they had the same legal effect as Regulations.

Nevertheless, the Court suggested that although Directives could not have horizontal direct effect, an individual would have other options of obtaining redress for alleged harm by pursuing their rights either through indirect effect or through the *Francovich* principles. (*See* under Member State Liability, p.36)

Direct Effect of Recommendations and Opinions
In *Grimaldi* [1989], Grimaldi suffered from what was classified as an occupational disease under a Recommendation but not under French law, thus depriving him of compensation through national proceedings. The Court made it clear that since the Treaty specified that Recommendations did not have binding legal effect, it would clearly be inappropriate for them to have direct effect. Grimaldi would therefore not be able to rely on the terms of the Recommendation.

As with Recommendations, Opinions do not have binding effect and the ruling in *Grimaldi* applies to them also.

Indirect Effect
Despite the Court's insistence that provisions of Community law must have *effet utile*, the main limitations on the direct effect of Directives are that legally binding European legislation:

- Must fulfil the *Van Gend en Loos* criteria—be sufficiently precise, unconditional and not involve discretion in the method of implementation;
- Cannot have direct effect until the time limit for implementation has expired;
- Cannot have direct effect unless a Member State has incorrectly implemented their provisions into national law; and
- Does not have horizontal direct effect.

The Court therefore created a obligation on national courts to interpret national law in such a way as to achieve the aim of the Directive. This approach—known as indirect effect—was based on Article 5 (now Article 10) which requires Member States to "take all appropriate measures, whether general or particular, to ensure fulfilment of the obligations arising out of this Treaty or resulting from action taken by the institutions of the Community."

In the case of *Von Colson und Kamman v Land Nordrhein-Westfalen* [1984] challenge was made under the Equal Treatment Directive 76/207. The Court of Justice found that the Directive was not sufficiently precise and unconditional to possess direct effect but invoked Article 5 which placed Member States under an obligation to fulfil their Treaty obligations, stating that national implementing legislation had to be sufficient "such as to guarantee real and effective judicial protection" and that "it was for the national court to interpret and apply the legislation adopted … in conformity with the requirements of Community law, in so far as it is given discretion to do so under national law".

This approach was extended in *Marleasing SA v La Commercial Internacional de Alimentacion SA* [1990] a case brought by one company against another. As well as reiterating the prohibition against horizontal direct effect, the Court repeated the obligation on national courts to interpret national legislation whether adopted before or after the Directive as far as possible in the light of the wording and purpose of the Directive.

The rulings in these cases have sometimes proved problematic for national courts obliged to interpret national legislation which predates a Directive, particularly in the UK (*Litster v Forth Dry Dock Engineering*

[1990]). The Court of Justice has also made it clear that indirect effect cannot be used in criminal proceedings (*Kolpinghuis Nijmegen* [1987]).

MEMBER STATE LIABILITY

After a series of cases in which horizontal direct effect was denied, the Court then turned in a different direction to protect individuals' Community rights. Individuals who had suffered as a result of a Member State's failure to fulfil its Community obligations had at that stage little redress in law, other than to rely on a national court making a preliminary reference to the European Court of Justice on the interpretation of the Treaty.

In 1991 with the landmark case of *Francovich*, it began to build a system of Member State liability to provide effective rights for individuals by placing an obligation upon a defaulting Member State to recompense individuals in damages for its own failure. Although in *Francovich*, Directive 80/987 (on the protection of workers in the event of the insolvency of their employer) was held not to be directly effective, the Court held that the protection of Community rights would be weakened if individuals were unable to obtain any effective remedy when their rights were infringed by a breach of Community law for which a Member State could be held responsible. It laid down three conditions to be fulfilled before a Member State might be found to be liable in damages even if the measure was not directly effective:

* The Directive must confer rights for the benefits of individuals;
* The content of the rights must be identifiable from the Directive; and
* There must be a causal link between the damage suffered and the breach.

The Court did not decide how the extent of liability was to be determined. This was to be a matter for the national courts to determine—though national procedures had "to ensure the full protection of rights which individuals might derive from Community law".

The implications of the *Francovich* judgment were that Member States faced the possibility of paying compensation to individuals if they failed to implement a Directive in time. But some areas of doubt remained; whether any other type of breach of Community law by Member States other than a failure to implement a Directive would lead to Member States incurring liability in damages; and secondly, whether "fault" was necessary in order to incur liability.

Where the Court has found a Member State to have a wide discretion, that is to say the competent national authorities have substantive choices in how they can act under Community law, it has applied the *Factortame* (No. 3) conditions. These were set out in joined cases *Brasserie du Pêcheur v Germany SA* [1996] and *R v Secretary of State for Transport, ex parte Factortame Ltd* [1991] in which the Court considered claims for compensation as a result of conflicting national and Community law. These conditions were that:

* The rule of law infringed must be intended to confer rights on individuals;
* The breach must be sufficiently serious; and

- There must be a direct causal link between the breach of the obligation resting on the state and the damage sustained by the injured parties.

The requirements for establishing state liability are clearly similar to those arising from Francovich with the added requirement of establishing a "sufficiently serious" breach. The Court clarified what it meant by this and provided guidelines for national courts to evaluate whether or not a breach was sufficiently serious as follows:

- How clear and precise was the rule which was breached?
- Did national authorities have any discretion in its implementation?
- Was the breach was intentional?
- Was the error of law excusable?
- Had a Community institution contributed to the breach?

The decisive test on whether or not a breach was sufficiently serious would be whether or not the Member State had manifestly and gravely disregarded the limits of its discretion.

In *R v Ministry of Agriculture, Fisheries and Food, ex parte Hedley Lomas (Ireland) Ltd* [1994] the Court applied the *Factortame (No. 3)* conditions. The Ministry of Agriculture, Fisheries and Food had refused licences for the exporting of livestock to Spain because it believed that Spain was acting contrary to Directive 74/557. The UK was held to have breached Community law by imposing an export ban contrary to Article 34 (now Article 29). It had clearly acted in the face of Community law and accordingly was liable in damages to Hedley Lomas.

In *R v HM Treasury, ex parte British Telecommunications plc* [1996] the issue was the incorrect implementation of a Directive by the UK where it clearly did not have wide discretion in its Community obligation to implement a Directive correctly. In this case though, the Directive at issue was imprecisely worded though the UK had acted in good faith. The breach was held not to be sufficiently serious enough to incur liability for damages.

However, in *Dillenkofer v Federal Republic of Germany* [1996] Germany had failed to implement Directive 90/314 in time. The type of breach was therefore similar to that in *Francovich*. The Court went on to apply the *Factortame (No. 3)* conditions rather than the original *Francovich* conditions, thus indicating that it regarded the conditions relating to state liability to be fixed no matter what the nature of the breach was. In this case, it stated that the very nature of Germany's breach of Community law—a complete disregard of its obligations—was sufficiently serious.

To provide an effective mechanism for the enforcement of individuals' rights, ensure consistent application of Community law throughout the Member States and to encourage Member States to be vigilant in their application of Community law the Court of Justice has now established that the requirements for state liability are that:

(1) Based on a Member State's obligations under Article 10 (ex Article 5) it must "take all appropriate measures … to ensure fulfilment of the obligations arising out of this Treaty … (and) facilitate the achievement of the Community's tasks. (It) shall abstain from any measure which could jeopardise the attainment of the objectives of this Treaty."

(2) A breach of Community law is *sufficiently serious* where, in the exercise of its legislative powers, a Member State has manifestly and gravely disregarded the limits on the exercise of its powers. If, at the time when it committed the infringement, the Member State in question did not have legislative choices and had only considerably reduced, or even no discretion, the mere infringement of Community law may be sufficient to establish the existence of a sufficiently serious breach.

(3) The nature of a sufficiently serious breach of a Member State's obligations does not necessarily require to be the non-implementation of a Directive. Such a breach could include instances of actions by a Member State:

- after a judgment by the Court finding it in breach of Community law;
- where it had persisted in its actions despite that judgment;
- where it had taken no action to implement a Directive; and
- where it had acted (or omitted to act) in the face of established Community law.

(4) Fault—whether negligent or intentional—is not in one of the conditions which it is necessary to satisfy in order for state liability to be established, especially since the concept of "fault" may differ throughout the various legal systems of the Member States.

(5) It is for the national courts to determine whether a breach of Community law is sufficiently serious to incur the non-contractual liability of a Member State vis-à-vis individuals.

SUPREMACY

Creating an effective legal system to apply directly within the Member States in a uniform and consistent manner would be of little value if Member States themselves could enact conflicting measures which would override Community law or choose which Community rules they would—or would not—apply. Nor were the founding Treaties of any assistance, as they contained no express provision on how to deal with the possibility of a conflict between a rule of Community law and national provisions. The basis of the Court's deduction of the supremacy of Community law therefore was to rely on Article 5 (now Article 10) of the Treaty which set out the obligations of the Member States to ensure its effectiveness and by implication, the effectiveness of legislation enacted in furtherance of Treaty objectives.

In the case of *Costa v ENEL* [1964], Mr Costa challenged a small electricity bill from the Italian State electricity authority, arguing that the Italian legislation nationalising the electricity industry infringed both the Italian Constitution and the provisions of the EEC Treaty. In a much-quoted statement, the Court held that:

"By creating a Community of unlimited duration, having its own institutions, its own personality, its own legal capacity and capacity of representation on the international plane and more particularly, real powers stemming from a limitation of sovereignty or a transfer of powers from the States of the Community, the Member States have limited their sovereign rights, albeit within limited fields, and have thus created a body of law which binds both their nationals and themselves.

The integration into the laws of each Member States of provisions which derive from the Community, and more generally the terms and the spirit of the Treaty *make it impossible for the States,* as a corollary, *to accord precedence to a unilateral and subsequent measure over a legal system accepted by them* [emphasis added]."

The supremacy of Community law was given further weight in *Internationale Handelsgesellschaft* [1970] and in *Simmenthal* [1977] in which the Court went further and stated that:

"Any National Court must ... apply Community law in its entirety... and must accordingly set aside any provision of national law which may conflict with it, whether prior or subsequent to the Community rule."

In the UK, the European Communities Act 1972 provides for the supremacy of Community law by accepting the legal effect of Community provisions in the UK. The same applies to judgments of the Court of Justice concerning interpretation on the meaning and effect, or validity of any Community measure. In relation to Acts of the UK Parliament, this means that directly applicable Community measures prevail even over future Acts of Parliament, if the latter are inconsistent with Community law. It also means that by ratifying the European Treaties, the UK, like any other Member State must refrain from enacting legislation inconsistent with Community Law. In 1991, in Factortame (No. 2) the Court of Justice replied to a question put by the UK House of Lords:

"Community law must be interpreted as meaning that a national court which, in a case before it concerning Community law, considers that the sole obstacle which precludes it from granting interim relief is a rule of national law, must set aside that rule."

Nevertheless, accepting supremacy of Community law—whether a Treaty Article, secondary legislation or agreement with a third state—raised difficulties in some Member States over the years, particularly with respect to previously enacted national law or the provisions of a Member State's own constitution.

The role of the Court of Justice was pivotal in settling the issues which arose. Interpreting Community law was entrusted by the Treaty solely to the Court and through its caselaw the concept of primacy of Community law now means that:

- States have agreed through their membership of the European Community to the limitation of their sovereign rights, *Costa v ENEL* [1964];
- Community law may not be invalidated by any provisions of national constitutions, *Internationale Handelsgesellschaft* [1970];
- Previously enacted but conflicting national law must be repealed, *Commission v France (re French Merchant Seamen)* [1974];

- Community law must be applied immediately without waiting for inconsistent national law to be repealed, *Simmenthal* [1977];
- Member States may not plead "force majeur", *Commission v Italy (Second Art Treasures case)* [1971];
- Supremacy applies regardless of whether the inconsistent national law is civil or criminal in nature, *Procureur du Roi v Dassonville* [1974];
- National courts should interpret national legislation so as to comply with the Member State's Community obligations whether the national law is passed before or after the relevant provision of Community law, *Marleasing* [1990]; and
- This obligation must not be applied retrospectively to penalise individuals, *Kolpinghuis Nijmegen* [1987].

SUBSIDIARITY

In an attempt to demonstrate that the relationship between Community law and national law was not one which irrevocably transferred the centre of power from national governments to Community institutions, in 1993 the Treaty on European Union formally introduced the principle of subsidiarity into the EC Treaty by inserting Article 3b (now Article 5) into the principles of the Community. It set out that

> "in areas which do not fall within its exclusive competence, the Community shall take action, in accordance with the principle of subsidiarity, only if and insofar as the objectives of the proposed action cannot be sufficiently achieved by Member States and can therefore by reason of the scale or effects of the proposed action, be better achieved by the Community."

In essence, this meant that the choice of legislative or other action would be directed in favour of Member States in cases where:

- Legislative or other action required to be taken by either the Member States or the Community;
- The Treaty did not specify that the Community possessed the power to act;
- The powers could be exercised by a Member State more effectively and in proportion to the objective pursued; and
- the need for action at Community level could not be demonstrated.

In the face of some confusion over aspects of the application of this principle, a Protocol on the Application of the Principles of Subsidiarity and Proportionality attached to the Treaty of Amsterdam set out that

> *"for Community action to be justified* both aspects of the subsidiarity principle shall be met: the objectives of the proposed action cannot be sufficiently achieved by Member States' action in the framework of their national constitutional system and can therefore be better achieved by action on the part of the Community. The following guidelines should be used in examining whether the abovementioned condition is fulfilled:
>
> - the issue under consideration has transnational aspects which cannot be satisfactorily regulation by action by Member States

- actions by Member States alone or lack of Community action would conflict with the requirements of the Treaty (such as the need to correct distortion of competition or avoid disguised restrictions on trade or strengthen economic and social cohesion) or would otherwise significantly damage Member States' interests
- action at Community level would produce clear benefits by reason of its scale or effects compared with action at the level of the Member States

The form of Community action shall be as simple as possible, consistent with satisfactory achievement of the objective of the measure and the need for effective enforcement. The Community shall legislate only to the extent necessary. Other things being equal, directives should be preferred to regulations and framework directives to detailed measures...

Regarding the nature and the extent of Community action, Community measures should leave as much scope for national decision as possible, consistent with securing the aim of the measure and observing the requirements of the Treaty ...

Where the application of the principle of subsidiarity leads to no action being taken by the Community, Member States are required in their action to comply with the general rules laid down in Article 5 (now Article 10) of the Treaty by taking all appropriate measures to ensure fulfilment of their obligations under the Treaty and by abstaining from any measure which could jeopardise the attainment of the objectives of the Treaty. [emphasis added]"

As the Institutions primarily concerned in the legislative process, the Commission, the Council and Parliament have express responsibility for demonstrating the effective application of this principle. For any provision which falls under the principle and after "consulting widely", the Commission must justify the relevance of its proposals with regard to subsidiarity and detail this in its Explanatory Memorandum. Compliance with Article 10 of Commission proposals must be specifically addressed by the Council and the European Parliament during the passage of legislation. In the preamble to the measure in question, reasons demonstrating its compliance with the principles of subsidiarity and proportionality must be set out.

Despite the Protocol, application of this Treaty provision has not been without its problems. Issues relating to its political relevance in the division of powers between the Community and its Member States and whether an action for judicial review can be founded on the issue of subsidiarity have still not been satisfactorily resolved.

---

7. JUDICIAL REVIEW

To protect the rights of individuals and Member States, the Treaty provides for an extensive system of judicial review to ensure that Community

Institutions fulfil their obligations under the Treaty in a proper manner. Based on French administrative law, judicial review also safeguards the rights of the Institutions in their dealings with one another. The Treaty confers specific powers and duties on each of the Institutions which they must exercise according to the Treaty:

- Under Article 230 (ex Article 173) the Court of Justice may consider an action for annulment of an act of the Institutions;
- Article 232 (ex Article 175) provides the means by which an Institution's failure to act may be investigated; and
- Article 241 (ex Article 184) provides a means of indirect review where the "plea of illegality" is invoked.

By far the most important of these three is the action for annulment under Article 230.

ACTION FOR ANNULMENT UNDER ARTICLE 230

Article 230

"The Court of Justice shall review the legality of acts adopted jointly by the European Parliament and the Council, of acts of the Council, of the Commission and of the ECB, other than recommendations and opinions, and of acts of the European Parliament intended to produce legal effects vis-à-vis third parties.

It shall for this purpose have jurisdiction in actions brought by a Member State, the Council or the Commission on grounds of lack of competence, infringement of an essential procedural requirement, infringement of this Treaty or of any rule of law relating to its application, or misuse of powers.

The Court shall have jurisdiction under the same conditions in actions brought by the European Parliament and by the ECB for the purpose of protecting their prerogatives.

Any natural or legal person may, under the same conditions, institution proceedings against a decision addressed to that person or against a decision which, although in the form of a regulation or a decision addressed to another person, is of direct and individual concern to the former.

The proceedings provided for in this Article shall be instituted within two months of the publication of the measure, or of its notification to the plaintiff, or, in the absence thereof, of the day on which it came to the knowledge of the latter, as the case may be."

In order to be successful, the action for annulment brought under Article 230 must clear two hurdles. The first is the admissibility requirement. This means that the applicant must first satisfy the Court that he or she (or it, in the case of a business) is allowed to bring the action in the first place and that it is within the time limits laid down. This is known as locus standi. Secondly, the applicant must then convince the Court that the challenge is on one of the grounds for review which is allowed under Article 230.

The Treaty of Nice which was signed on February 26, 2001 (but not yet in force), will confer jurisdiction on the Court of First Instance to hear most classes of direct actions such as in Article 230 (Annulment), Article 232 (Failure to Act), Article 235 (Non-contractual Liability of the Community), Article 236 (Staff Cases) and Article 238 (Arbitration Clauses). Actions brought by the Member States, the institutions and the European Central Bank are reserved for the Court of Justice.

To found a successful action, five questions must be addressed.

(1) What Acts may be Challenged?

Anything which is legally binding—Regulations, Decisions, Directives. But not Recommendations and Opinions (see Article 249). However, these forms of legislation are not all that may be challenged. Because the Court of Justice is concerned with the substance of a measure rather than the form it takes, it will consider all measures taken by the Institutions which are designed to have legal effect. In *Commission v Council (re ERTA)* [1971], "discussions" of guidelines before the signing of the European Road Traffic Agreement were held to be capable of review by the Court. More recently, in *European Parliament v Council* [1994] the Court stated that

> "annulment must be available in the case of all measures adopted by the institutions, whatever their nature or form, intended to have legal effects. It follows that an action … is admissible irrespective of whether the act was adopted by the institution pursuant to the Treaty provisions."

However in *IBM v Commission* [1981], the company challenged a letter and Statement of Objections sent by the Commission in pursuance of competition rules. As this was only the first step of several in an enforcement procedure the Court held that this could not be challenged. Only a final measure may be challenged.

(2) Who has the Right to Challenge?

A distinction is drawn between institutional and private applicants—between what are referred to as privileged applicants, limited privileged applicants and non-privileged applicants.

Privileged applicants are the Member States, the Council, and the Commission. They have an automatic right to challenge any legal measure as they are presumed to have an interest in any Community proceedings (*Luxembourg v European Parliament* [1983]).

Limited privileged applicants are the Parliament, the European Central Bank and the Court of Auditors. They have a limited right to challenge measures, but only if they can demonstrate a specific interest in the proceedings and to safeguard their powers (*European Parliament v Council* [1991]).

Private individuals and companies (natural or legal persons)—that is, non-privileged applicants—may challenge a Community act but only if this act is:

- A Decision addressed to that person. This means that there is an obvious and straightforward right of challenge. If the addressee of the contested decision brings an action within the time limit, the claim will be admissible.

- A Decision addressed to another person or to a Member State. In this case, the applicant must show that the act in question is of direct and individual concern to them (*Fiskano v Commission* [1994]).
- A Decision in the form of a Regulation. As can be deduced from Article 249, a Regulation has "general application", that is, it applies not to a limited number of people, but a wide range, defined abstractly and unnamed. A "true" Regulation may not be challenged (*Calpack* [1980]). Only Decisions have the characteristic of binding those to whom they are addressed. Even if the measure is in the form of a Regulation, it must be equivalent to a Decision and apply to identifiable individuals and once more, it must be of direct and individual concern to the applicant (*International Fruit Co. v Commission* [1970]).

Having established that the individual is in fact challenging a Decision (or a Decision in the form of a Regulation), the next step is to establish direct and individual concern.

A measure is of direct concern to an applicant when a Member State is given no discretion to act under the disputed provision or when there is no implementing measure required to be acted upon by the Member State. In *Bock* [1971] despite the fact that the German authorities had already informed the applicant that they would reject his application for an import licence for Chinese mushrooms as soon as the Commission allowed them to do so, it was held that Germany's discretion whether or not to authorise the import licence was not at issue as the Commission had upheld a refusal in response to Bock's application. Bock was held to be directly concerned.

It is of individual concern if it affects the applicant in the same way as if it had been addressed to him personally, either alone or as a member of a closed class. The test is that in *Plaumann* [1963]. Plaumann was a fruit importer. A Decision sent by the Commission to Germany refused permission to reduce the duty on clementines imported from outside the Community. Plaumann challenged the Commission's decision. That his business would be affected was not sufficient to constitute "individual concern" within the meaning of Article 230. The Court said the measure was a response to a general problem and drafted accordingly, without special reference to any individual trader, present or potential. Plaumann was merely an importer and as anyone could set up in business as an importer, Plaumann was not therefore individually concerned.

Although most applicants seeking to prove individual concern are unsuccessful, in the case of *Töpfer*, an importer of grain and cereals had requested a licence on October 1, 1963 from the German Government so that he could import cereals from France. He was refused permission and the Commission was asked to confirm this decision which it did, retrospectively, on October 4. The Court said that the identity of the applicant had been known to the Commission before October 4, and it was therefore in a position to know that its decision affected the interests of existing importers. This fact distinguished Töpfer, he was therefore individually concerned and accordingly his action was admissible.

In *Bock's* case in 1971, the Court held that the company was individually concerned because the application made to import Chinese mushrooms was made on September 11, refused by Germany on the same date but upheld by the Commission on September 15. The number and identity of importers concerned was already fixed and ascertainable before the refusal by the Commission on September 15, and it was in a position to know that its decision would affect the interests and situation of those importers alone.

The 1985 case of *Piraiki-Patriki* concerned seven Greek cotton companies which challenged a Commission Decision allowing the French Government to impose a quota system on imports of yarn from Greece between November 1981 and January 1982. Some of the applicants had already signed contracts with French companies for deliveries above the quota during that period. The Court held that the decision was of individual concern to those of the applicants who had signed the contracts as they were "members of a limited class of traders identified or identifiable by the Commission and by reason of these contracts, particularly affected by the decision."

However, in the case of *Codorniu* in 1994 the Court of Justice developed its approach to "individual concern" further. The measure in question was in the form of a Regulation made by the Council which reserved the term crémant for particular types of sparkling wine produced in France and Luxembourg. The applicant was a major producer of sparkling wines in Spain, one of the largest producers of sparkling wine in Europe and had held a Spanish trademark since 1924 for its Gran Crémant wine. The Court held that the measure was a true Regulation of general application and although Codorniu was not one of a fixed and ascertainable group he was distinguished from other producers as he would be deprived of the trademark right which he had held for the previous 70 years.

The Court reverted to its more restrictive approach as set out in *Plaumann* in the case of *Stichtung Greenpeace Council* in 1998 which seemed to indicate that it was still difficult to get past the *locus standi* hurdle. Greenpeace had challenged a Commission Decision to allocate financial aid to Spain to build two power stations in the Canary Islands on environmental grounds. The Court held that "the interests [of the local residents, fishermen and farmers] are by their very nature, common and shared, and the rights relating to these are liable to be held by a potentially large number of individuals so there could never be a closed class of applicants".

These restrictive rules on locus standi for private applicants have been unchanged since 1958, despite the Courts own misgivings about their continuance, set out in its submission to the 1996 IGC. And this made it almost impossible for an individual to pass the admissibility test for a challenge under Article 230. Nevertheless in the case of *Jégo-Quéré et Cie* [2002] the Court of First Instance deviated from the past case law and relaxed its previous restrictive application of 'individual concern' of a Regulation, only to have it made crystal clear to it by the Court of Justice later in the year in *Unión de Pequeños Agricultores*[2002] when it held (against the advice of the Advocate General in the case) that the pre-*Jégo-Quéré* caselaw was still to apply. It emphasised that it was not for the Court to reform the conditions for locus standi and that if Member States wished to extend the rights of individuals to challenge Community measures by changing the law, their amendment of the Treaty would be the only way.

(3) What are the Grounds for Challenge?

Lack of Competence
The Treaty requires each of the Community institutions to act within the limits of the powers conferred upon it. Thus in the *ERTA* case [1989], it was obvious to the Court that the Council lacked the power to negotiate the European Road Transport Agreement, as Article 228 (now Article 300) states that the Commission negotiates international agreements and the Council concludes them. It follows that every act of a Community institution must clearly indicate on which Treaty provision it is based. To date, the Member States have declined to take up this option.

Infringement of an Essential Procedural Requirement
Institutions adopting binding measures must adhere to the correct procedures as laid down either in the Treaty or within secondary legislation implemented in accordance with the Treaty. The leading case, *Roquette Frères* [1980] concerned a requirement for Parliament to be consulted in a legal measure. "Failure to consult" annulled the measure in question.

"Failure to give sufficient reasons" may also be grounds for annulment of a binding measure This ground of review is normally pleaded when an institution has not given reasons for its adoption of binding legal measures (*Commission v Council Re Titanium Dioxide Waste* [1991]). The measure must therefore specify the principal issues of fact and law in a clear and concise manner so that the reasoning which led the institution to make its choice of legal basis may be clearly understood.

Infringement of the Treaty or of any Rule Relating to its Application
This ground of challenge is interpreted broadly because it covers not only the Treaties and their implementing legislation, but also general principles of law such as:

- Equality (*R Louwage v Commission* [1974]);
- Legal certainty (*Openbaar Ministerie v Bout* [1982]);
- Proportionality (*Commission v Germany* [1994]);
- Fundamental rights (now expressly set out in Article 6(1) of the Treaty on European Union); and
- Legitimate expectation (*Töpfer* [1965]).

Misuse of Powers
This refers to an act of an institution endeavouring to achieve an objective which is not that for which the original powers were conferred upon it. The Court will examine:

- The purpose the act was intended to achieve; and
- The purpose of the provision under which the act was adopted, to see if the act followed this purpose.

This ground is the most difficult to prove as evidence is required that the intention of the institution in question was different from that stated in the contested measure (*Crispoltoni* [1994]).

(4) What are the Relevant Time Limits?

The Court enforces the time limits very strictly. An applicant—whether privileged or non-privileged, must bring a claim within two months of the date of publication, or the date it was notified to the pursuer or the date he became aware of it. This two-month time limit is extended to take account of the distance of the applicant from the Court in Luxembourg. A 10-day extension is granted for the UK. A further 14-day extension comes into effect when the measure is published in the Official Journal.

Regulations, Directives and Decisions adopted in accordance with the co-decision procedure must be published in the Official Journal along with Council and Commission Regulations and Directives of these institutions which are addressed to all Member States. Other Directives and Decisions only require to be notified to those to whom they are addressed. They enter into force on the day specified in the act or if this is not specified, on the twentieth day following publication.

If there is no challenge within the time limit, the measure is "good forever" and any challenge is inadmissible.

(5) What are the Consequences of Annulment?

Article 231 (ex Article 174) provides that if the action brought under Article 230 is successful the Court shall declare the measure void from the very beginning. The Court has no power to order the institution concerned to take any particular steps but it is required under Article 233 (ex Article 176) to take the measures necessary to comply with the Court's judgment and therefore to endeavour to recreate the situation which would have existed had the measure not been adopted.

If the measure is a Regulation, only the offending parts may be annulled (Article 231(2)). (*Société de Vente de Ciments et Bétons v Kerpen & Kerpen* [1983]), **or**, the offending measure can remain in force until a new one is in force (*Timex v Council* [1985]), **or**, to preserve legal certainty the annulment only applies to the parties concerned in the case (*Simmenthal* [1979]).

APPEAL AGAINST FAILURE OF AN INSTITUTION TO ACT UNDER ARTICLE 232

Article 232

"Should the European Parliament, the Council or the Commission, in infringement of this Treaty, fail to act, the Member States and the other institutions of the Community may bring an action before the Court of Justice to have the infringement established.

This action shall be admissible only if the institution concerned has first been called upon to act. If, within two months of being so called upon, the institution concerned has not defined its position, the action may be brought within a further period of two months.

Any natural or legal person may, under the conditions laid down in the preceding paragraphs, complain to the Court of Justice that an institution of the Community has failed to address to that person any act other than a recommendation or an opinion.

The Court of Justice shall have jurisdiction, under the same conditions, in actions or proceedings brought by the ECB in the areas falling within the latter's field of competence and in actions or proceedings brought against the latter."

(1) What may be Challenged?
Actions under Article 232 can be regarded as 'the other side of the coin' from actions under Article 230. While judicial review under Article 230 may annul acts of the institutions, failure to act under Article 232 may be used to compel an institution to fulfil its Community obligations. An action will thus *only be available where the applicant can show that such an obligation exists.*

The action for failure to act on the part of the European Parliament, the Council or the Commission can also be pleaded in the same action as that for annulment under Article 230. An apparent inconsistency between the two can be resolved by applying the "unity principle" whereby the Court has stated that "both provisions merely prescribe one and the same method of recourse" (*Chevalley v Commission* [1970]).

(2) Who has the Right to Challenge?
As with Article 230, there is a distinction between the status of applicants. In this case, Parliament is placed on the same footing as Member States and the right of action is given to "other institutions" of the Community. Individuals may only challenge a failure to act when it concerns a binding act of which they would have been the addressee (*Mackprang v Commission* [1971]) and in which they are able to establish direct and individual concern (*ENU v Commission* [1993]).

(3) What are the Relevant Time Limits?
Although the Treaty does not specify any time limit during which an action must be initiated, the applicant must approach the institution concerned beforehand and make it quite clear that if, within a two-month time limit, it does not comply with its Community obligations to act, it will be subject to a challenge under Article 232. Once this approach has been made the institution concerned has a period of two months within which to define its position. If it does not do this, the applicant has a further two months within which to bring the action.

(5) What are the Consequences of a Successful Challenge?
If the application under Article 232 is upheld, the Court will declare that the failure to act is contrary to the Treaty and Article 233 (ex Article 176) requires that the institution must "take the necessary measures to comply with the judgment of the Court of Justice" within a reasonable period of time. If, however, the Institution has defined its position but not adopted the disputed measure, it is not possible to bring an action for "failure to act" (*Lütticke* [1966]).

PLEA OF ILLEGALITY UNDER ARTICLE 241

Article 241

"Notwithstanding the expiry of the period laid down in ... Article 230, any party, may, in proceedings in which a regulation adopted jointly by the European Parliament and the Council, or a regulation of the Council, of the Commission, or of the ECB is at issue, plead the grounds specified in ... Article 230 in order to invoke before the Court of Justice the inapplicability of that regulation."

This Treaty Article also provides for a challenge to the act of an institution, in this case, a Regulation. Unlike Articles 230 and 232, a plea of illegality under Article 241 is an indirect action. It is only available as a defence where other proceedings have been brought against the applicant and may be pleaded only in the course of proceedings which are already underway on other grounds. Because of the restrictive nature of locus standi for the action of annulment under Article 230, the individual may not mount a direct challenge to a Regulation. However, in the course of Article 230 proceedings challenging a Decision, provided he overcomes the admissibility hurdle, he may claim that the original Regulation on which the Decision is based, is illegal. This action has also been held to covers acts of the institutions which produce similar effects to those of Regulations but which do not actually take the form of Regulations (*Simmenthal* [1979]).

If the Article 241 plea succeeds, although the Regulation itself will not be annulled, its basis for the Decision in question will be "inapplicable" and the Decision will be void.

---

8. PRELIMINARY RULINGS

Giving effect to Community law as set out by the Treaties and ensuring its provisions would be applied throughout the Member States by all national courts in a uniform and consistent manner was essential to the authors of the Community Treaties if the proper functioning of the common market was to be achieved and preserved. To that end, Article 234 (ex Article 177) enables national courts and tribunals to refer questions of Community law that require to be decided in a case pending before them to the Court of Justice for a ruling. This procedure has also proved to be the springboard for the development of some of the most fundamental concepts of Community law, such as direct effect and supremacy.

Notwithstanding the advances made for the benefit of individuals seeking to enforce their Community rights within their own national courts through the doctrine of direct effect, the preliminary ruling procedure has allowed them to mount challenges to the validity of Community acts in a manner which is much less restrictive than the procedural requirements of judicial review.

This preliminary rulings procedure is not one which an individual may use to bring his case direct. It is an "indirect action". It involves the national court hearing a case concerning a point of Community law and asking for guidance on its interpretation from the Court of Justice. The Court of First Instance has no jurisdiction in this particular procedure. The system of preliminary rulings represents a dialogue between a national court and the Court of Justice. The parties in the case cannot ask a national judge to make a request for a preliminary ruling to Luxembourg.

The procedure involves a national court seeking guidance on a point of interpretation, or validity of European law by formulating a question (or questions) for clarification by the Court of Justice. The case in the national court is then suspended until a ruling is given. The Court of Justice does not investigate the facts of the case, nor does it apply the law to the case. It simply clarifies the point of European law. The judgment is binding on the national court referring the question which then continues the case and in due course, gives judgment in the light of the European Court's interpretation of the law.

Article 234 itself provides a great deal of information on who may use it and when questions should be referred. It reads as follows:

> "The Court of Justice shall have jurisdiction to give preliminary rulings concerning the interpretation of this Treaty; the validity and interpretation of acts of the institutions of the Community and of the ECB; the interpretation of the statutes of bodies established by an act of the Council, where those statutes so provide.
>
> Where such a question is raised before any court or tribunal of a Member State, that court or tribunal may, if it considers that a decision on the question is necessary to enable it to give judgment, request the Court of Justice to give a ruling thereon.
>
> Where any such question is raised in a case pending before a court or tribunal of a Member State against whose decisions there is no judicial remedy under national law, that court or tribunal shall bring the matter before the Court of Justice."

The power of the Court therefore falls into two main groups, first is the Court's interpretation of Community law and secondly is its power to rule on the on the validity of the acts of the institutions.

THE INTERPRETATION OF COMMUNITY LAW

Under Article 234(1) the Court of Justice has jurisdiction to interpret:

*   The Treaties (European Coal and Steel Community Treaty, the European Community Treaty and the Euratom Treaty);
*   All the Acts of the Institutions, whether legally binding or not; and
*   International agreements which are concluded by the Community with third countries.

The main interpretative techniques of the Court of Justice are contextual and teleological. Though it always starts with the text of the Treaty and places the object and purpose of the provision in question within its context in relation to other provisions, the Court may also look at the general scheme of the Treaty as a whole and at its broad policy objectives, even though these are in the main set out in very general terms.

THE VALIDITY OF THE ACTS OF THE INSTITUTIONS

According to the judgment in *Grad* [1970] national courts are empowered to submit to the European Court all questions regarding validity of all measures without distinction. The Court can therefore rule on the validity of Regulations, Directives, Decisions, Recommendations and Opinions.

Although the wording of Article 234(1) mentions "validity", Article 230 governing the system of judicial review concerns "legality" and so with these two Articles the Court has created a complete system of legal remedies to review all the acts of the institutions (*Les Verts v European Parliament* [1986]).

Unlike the four grounds of review under Article 230, Article 234 does not contain any restrictions as to grounds on which validity of Community acts may be contested (*International Fruit Co. (No. 3)* [1972]).

As opposed to the time limitation by which cases for judicial review may be lodged, questions of validity may be raised under Article 234 at any time.

The finding of the Court through a preliminary ruling is binding on the parties to the case in the national courts, but if an act of an institution is declared invalid, it is normally retroactive as under Article 230 from when the act was originally adopted. If it is declared invalid, it is invalid throughout the Community.

There is nothing in the wording of Article 234 to say who may declare a Community act invalid. In the case of *Foto-Frost* [1987], the Court stated that national courts may consider the validity of a Community act. If is clearly valid they may make a statement to this effect, though a national court cannot declare a Community act to be invalid. As a requirement of legal certainty, this is a prerogative of the Court of Justice which it will exercise through the preliminary ruling procedure.

Article 234(2) contains the provision for an optional or discretionary reference to the Court of Justice. When a matter comes before a national court it may refer a question though it is not obliged to do so.

"Where such a question is raised before any court or tribunal of a member state, that court or tribunal may, if it considers that a decision on the question is necessary to enable it to give judgement, request the Court of Justice to give a ruling thereon."

The national court must therefore establish the facts of the case before it. If an issue of Community law is critical to its final determination of the case and it does not have complete confidence in its ability to resolve the issue itself it should refer the question to the Court of Justice. It should bear in mind the differences between national and Community legislation, the need for uniform interpretation throughout the Community and of the great advantages enjoyed by the Court of Justice in construing Community measures (*R v International Stock Exchange ex parte Else* [1993]).

The Court of Justice does not enquire into the reasons why the national court has made a reference (*Costa v ENEL*) but in the case of *Foglia v Novello* [1980], it stated that it had a duty to give national courts information to decide real disputes between parties, but would not decide artificial or hypothetical ones. If it were to do this, it would jeopardise the whole purpose of Article 234.

As a matter of Community law, national courts have an absolute and unfettered discretion to refer which cannot be removed. Thus any attempt to influence the courts in this matter by Parliament or government would be unlawful.

In Article 234 (3), there is provision for a compulsory reference:

> "Where any such question is raised before any court or tribunal of a member state against whose decisions there is no judicial remedy under national law, that court or tribunal shall bring the matter before the Court of Justice."

The difference in the two paragraphs hinges on the words "may" and "shall". "May" means it is optional, at the discretion of the national court and "shall" conveys the imperative.

With a compulsory reference, the key words are "a court against whose decisions there is no judicial remedy". In these cases, if a question of Community law—interpretation or validity of a measure—is raised before a court from which there is no appeal, then that court is bound to send a question to the European Court. The purpose of this goes to the heart of Article 234. It will avoid a mistaken interpretation of Community law being given by the highest courts in the land other courts being bound by that decision through the doctrine of precedent. In other words, it prevents a body of national caselaw coming into existence in any Member State which is not in accordance with Community law. And, as with the whole of Article 234, it ensures the uniform interpretation and application of the law.

A compulsory referral from a court from which there is no appeal is also ensures that if a lower court has not made a reference to the Court of Justice—which it is perfectly entitled to do under Article 234(2)—this is the final stage where any errors of law can be corrected.

So which actual courts in a member state are subject to the obligation to refer? The problems which have arisen in this respect have led to the development of two theories:

(1) Only national courts which are always a court of last resort in the hierarchy of judicial precedent. For example, in Scotland the House of Lords for civil matters. This is the abstract theory.

(2) Any court which is a court of last resort in the case in question. This would include for example cases in the English Court of Appeal or the Scottish Court of Session when leave of appeal to the House of Lords has been refused. This is known as the concrete theory. (See *R v Henn and Derby* [1979]).

Article 234(2) also mentions the words "any court or tribunal". When is a body a court or tribunal, and when is it not? Cases have come to the European Court from quasi-judicial bodies and the question was to establish their *locus standi*—whether or not they were allowed even to refer a case to the Court of Justice.

Courts of law within the judicial hierarchy of a Member State have automatic status. Whether other bodies such as arbitration tribunals and appeals committees, for example, had *locus standi* was more problematic. In the case of *Walter Schmid* [2002] the Court of Justice set out the essential characteristics of a "court or tribunal" within the Community context. The criteria to be used to measure whether this was so were that the body:

- Is established by law;
- Is permanent;
- Has compulsory jurisdiction;
- Its procedure is *inter pares;*
- Applies the rule of law; and
- Is independent.

The right to refer questions to the Court of Justice belongs to national "courts or tribunals" only. Parliaments, governments and Community institutions do not have *locus standi* to submit a questions for preliminary rulings.

Article 234(3) down obligatory referral in cases where there "is no judicial remedy". National supreme courts are understandably reluctant to constantly refer questions on issues where they believe the European Court has already clarified the point. The Court of Justice itself has recognised that there may be occasions where it is not necessary to make a preliminary ruling. This relaxation of the strict nature of Article 234(3), *acte clair*, is based on French administrative law. It means that no question of interpretation of necessary where a provision is quite clear. The Court described the circumstances in which a national court need not refer a question in the case of *CILFIT* [1982]:

- Where a question of Community law is irrelevant to the case at issue;
- The point has already been decided by a previous decision of the Court of Justice;
- If the correct application of Community law is so obvious as to leave no doubt as to the manner in which the matter is to be resolved; and
- The matter is equally obvious to the Courts of the other Member States and to the Court of Justice.

The Court went on to set out the problems were a national supreme court to decide not to ask for a preliminary ruling in these circumstances:

- Community law is drafted in several different languages all of them equally authentic and binding, so any interpretation by a national court would require a comparison of all different language versions;
- Community law has its own particular terminology, legal concepts do not necessary have the same meaning in Community law as they do in national law; and
- Community law must always be interpreted in context and in the light of the purposes of the treaties as a whole, of the objectives of Community law and the evolution of Community law at that particular time, in other words, interpretation is by the teleological method.

Now that Community law is becoming more and more familiar to national judges, it is not unusual for the national supreme courts to use the doctrine of *acte clair* and decide cases containing a point of Community law without referring to the Court in Luxembourg (*British Fuels v Baxendale* [1999]).

To ensure that national courts are fully aware of the circumstances and the manner in which references should be made under Article 234, the Court of Justice issued a Note of Guidance on References by National Courts for Preliminary Rulings in December 1996 [1997] 1 C.M.L.R. 78. This Note of Guidance is not legally binding, but it summarises the caselaw of the Court and sets out a clear indication of how a case ought to be prepared for reference by a national court.

In 2000 the Rules of Procedure of the Court of Justice were amended ([2000] O.J. L122/43). There is now a simplified procedure for questions referred by a national court which are identical to questions that have already been answered where the answer to the question can be clearly deduced from existing caselaw or where the answer admits of no reasonable doubt. In these cases the Court of Justice may give its decision by reasoned order. It may also:

- Request from the parties all such information relating to the facts and any other relevant documents; and
- Request clarification from national courts which refer questions to It for a preliminary ruling.

The Court has also set up an accelerated procedure where a matter is considered to be of exceptional urgency to restrict the matters requiring a ruling to essential points of law.

The effect of a preliminary ruling is to bind the national court in the case in which the reference was made and any other national court considering the same point of law.

The preliminary rulings procedure:

- Gives individuals the opportunity for an indirect challenge to the validity of Community law within their own national courts;
- Allows an individual to obtain domestic remedies which would otherwise not be available in the event of a direct challenge under Article 230;
- Is a Court-to-Court dialogue only;
- Provides guidance to a national court when applying the law;
- Is not an appeals procedure;
- Allows Community to be interpreted by one authoritative source in a consistent and uniform manner throughout all Member States;
- Has allowed the Court of Justice to extend the scope and effectiveness of the Community legal order;
- Is not limited to the four grounds of view essential under Article 230;
- May be raised by a national court at any time;
- Must be raised by a national court or tribunal (within the Community context) unless the national court applies the *acte clair* doctrine; and
- Binds the court or tribunal which made the reference to the Court of Justice.

9. FREE MOVEMENT OF GOODS

Customs duties represent one of the oldest forms of national trade protection so it was hardly surprising that these and other such charges were one of the first obstacles to trade that the Treaty set about removing to create a Europe-wide internal market based on unimpeded movement of goods across the whole Community. Ensuring the free movement of goods is an area of law illustrating how the Court and the Community legislators—the Commission, the Parliament and the Council—combine to attain a fundamental objective of the Community.

Article 3(a) sets out

> "For the purposes set out in Article 2, the activities of the Community shall include ... the prohibition, as between Member States of customs duties and quantitative restrictions on the import and export of goods and of all other measures having equivalent effect".

This aim of establishing an integrated market can easily be frustrated by Member States practising forms of protectionism designed to shield their national industries from the competitive pressures of imports. The most obvious way in which this is done is by making imports more expensive or setting invisible barriers such as different product, consumer and environmental standards. In order to prohibit these and other protectionist practices, the Treaty has identified three areas to guard against Member States erecting barriers to free movement of goods. The rules apply both to goods which originate in a Member State and to those which come from a third country and are in free circulation within a Member State.

Although the prohibitions restricting free movement of goods are addressed to Member States, the most important Articles of the Treaty within the area of free movement of goods are directly effective (*Van Gend en Loos* [1963]).

These three areas are prohibitions on:

- The imposition of customs duties (tariffs) AND charges having equivalent effect to customs duties—Article 3(a), Article 23 (ex Article 9) and Article 25 (ex Article 12);
- Discriminatory internal taxation—Article 90 (ex Article 95); and
- quantitative restrictions on imports and exports (bans and quotas) AND measures having an equivalent effect to quantitative restrictions—Article 3(a), Article 28 (ex Article 30), Article 20 (ex Article 31), 30 (ex Article 36) and Article 95 (ex Article 100a).

CUSTOMS DUTIES AND CHARGES HAVING EQUIVALENT EFFECT TO CUSTOMS DUTIES

Article 23

"(1) The Community shall be based upon a customs union which shall cover all trade in goods and which shall involve the prohibition between

Member States of customs duties on imports and exports and of all charges having equivalent effect, and the adoption of a common customs tariff in their relations with third countries.

(2)The provisions of Article 25 and of Chapter 2 of this Title shall apply to products originating in Member States and to products coming from third countries which are in free circulation in Member States."

Externally, Article 23 refers to the Common Customs Tariff. Whenever goods cross an external border, the Common Customs Tariff is the same (set out in Commission Regulation 2658/87 which is regularly updated). Once it is paid, then the goods are in free circulation throughout the Member States. Member States do not have jurisdiction over the duty levied on goods from third countries. They may not amend the rate nor may they keep the proceeds which now belong to the Community as "own resources". Modification or suspension of the Common Customs Tariff is an exclusive Community matter and is decided by the Council.

From an internal, Community perspective, Article 23 means that Member States must abolish two types of measures:

• Customs duties on imports and exports; and
• Charges having equivalent effect to customs duties (CEEs).

Article 23 also mentions "goods", a term which is not defined in the Treaty. In *Commission v Italy* ((*re Export Tax on Art Treasures*) [1968]), Italy levied charges on the export of its national artistic heritage. It was held that these constituted goods as "products which can be valued in money and which are capable, as such, of forming the subject of commercial transactions." In *Thompson* [1978] the term "goods" was held to cover gold and silver collectors' coins provided they were not in circulation as legal tender.

Article 25 prohibits customs duties on imports and exports:

"Customs duties on imports and exports and charges having equivalent effect shall be prohibited between Member States. This prohibition shall also apply to customs duties of a fiscal nature."

In *Commission v Italy (re Export Tax on Art Treasures)* the Court stated that in view of its fundamental nature there could only be express exceptions to this prohibition and such exceptions would be interpreted strictly.

What are Customs Charges?
Customs charges are taxes, duties, and tariffs levied by the Member State whenever goods cross borders.

What are "charges having an equivalent effect to customs duties"?
The Treaty does not define this term but it was held by the Court in 1966 (*Germany v Commission*) to mean in this case, charges imposed on imports of agricultural products in the guise of administrative fees imposed in exchange for tasks undertaken by the authorities in the interest of, and at the request of individuals. The Court ruled that they were still unilateral measures, imposed by the state of its own volition which, regardless of their label and the means by which they were introduced, had the same

discriminatory and protective effect as customs duties. In other words, the name of the charge was not important; it was the effect that mattered. Accordingly, the action by Germany was dismissed.

The *Bauhuis* case in 1977 gave the most complete definition. The Court said that

> "any pecuniary charge—whatever its assignation and mode of application, which is levied unilaterally on goods by reason of the fact that they cross the frontier and which is not a customs duty in the strict sense, constitutes a charge with equivalent effect unless it relates to a general system of internal taxation applied systematically in accordance with the same criteria and at the same stage of marketing to domestic products alike."

Charges—no matter what they are called, or for what purpose—levied by a state solely because goods cross frontiers are charges having an equivalent effect to a customs duty, and therefore prohibited. The restrictive effect on trade between Member States of the Community that such charges engendered was prohibited.

In *Commission v Italy (re Statistical Levy)* in 1969, Italy imposed a charge on exported goods with the ostensible purpose of collecting statistical material to analyse trade patterns. The Court said that

> "any pecuniary charge, however small, and whatever its designation and mode of application, which is imposed unilaterally on domestic and foreign goods by reason of the fact that they cross a frontier, constitutes a charge even if it is not imposed for the benefit of the state, is not discriminatory or protective in effect and if the product on which the charge is imposed is not in competition with any domestic product."

The Court's attitude was:

- The Treaty was not to be circumvented by the form in which the charge was imposed (the form of the charge is irrelevant, the effect on trade between Member States is all important);
- The prohibition applied whether the duties were discriminatory or not;
- Whether or not the product on which the charge was imposed was in competition with domestic goods; and
- There were to be no exceptions.

In the case of *Sociaal Fonds voor Diamantarbeiders v S A Brachfeld & Sons (the Diamond Workers case)* in 1969, Belgium levied a tax on imported diamonds which would provide social security benefits for diamond workers. Again, the Court emphasised that such charges were prohibited, irrespective of their purpose. The prohibited effect would constitute an obstacle to the free movement of goods.

What if a Fee is Charged in Respect of some Service Given?
The service in question could be for a health inspection, a quality check or off-loading charge. The Court accepts that a member state is allowed to charge a fee for services provided to an importer. But such a charge is not to

be levied simply because goods cross a frontier. It must be for services rendered before it is lawful.

However, the service in question must be specific and must benefit the individual importer, unlike the statistical information collected in *Commission v Italy (re Statistical Levy)* which the Court considered to be of benefit to the whole economy. The Court also took a similar approach in *Bresciani* [1976] where the question was whether an Italian charge for compulsory veterinary and public health inspections carried out on the importation of raw cowhides, was compatible with the Treaty. The submissions in *Bresciani* as well as in the *Statistical Levy* case were rejected.

If a charge is for a specific inspection, benefiting the individual importer, then it falls outside the prohibition. But there is a condition—the service rendered must be mandatory. In *Commission v Germany (re Animal Inspection Fees)* [1988] the German authorities charged fees on imports of live animals. The revenue gained was to cover the cost of inspections required to comply with Directive 81/389. Under Community law, the Germany was obliged to achieve the result set out in the Directive by enacting its own legislation. The inspections were mandatory.

Charges for services authorised by Community law do not constitute charges having an equivalent effect to customs duties as long as they satisfy four conditions:

(1) The fee must not exceed the actual cost of the services rendered;
(2) The service must be uniform, that is applying both to imports and domestic products;
(3) The service is prescribed by Community law—a mandatory requirement—in the general interest of the Community; and
(4) The service promotes the free movement of goods.

These conditions are very strict. If fees are charged on any inspection which is not mandatory under Community law, this constitutes an obstacle to the free movement of goods and is unlawful. Charges which cannot satisfy the conditions are classified as charges having equivalent effect to a customs duty and prohibited under Article 25 (*Commission v Germany (re Animal Inspection Fees)* [1988]).

DISCRIMINATORY INTERNAL TAXATION

This is the second of the three sets of provisions within the Treaty to guarantee the free movement of goods and these rules also relates to monetary charges levied by a Member State. Whilst Articles 23 and 25 prevent financial measures in the form of customs duties at the borders of Member States it would defeat the aim of guaranteeing the abolition of charges if a Member State could then discriminate against imported goods once they were inside the borders. Article 90 is the main Treaty provision to prevent a state from placing a fiscal disadvantage in the way of imported goods in competition with domestic goods, once they are within the state by ensuring that the internal taxation system of a Member State makes no distinction between imported and domestic products.

What distinguishes discriminatory internal taxation from a charge having equivalent effect to a customs duty is that:

- Discriminatory internal taxation is imposed on *both* imported and domestic products; and
- Charges having equivalent effect to customs duties are imposed exclusively on the imported product.

Article 90

"No Member State shall impose, directly or indirectly, on the products of other Member States any internal taxation of any kind in excess of that imposed directly or indirectly to similar domestic products.

  Furthermore, no Member State shall impose on the products of other Member States any internal taxation of such a nature as to afford indirect protection to other products."

Article 90(1) deals with imported products which are so similar to domestic products that they require the same tax treatment. The important point is that the goods do not need to be identical, they only need to be similar. The term "similar" has been defined as products which are broadly in competition with one another, "with similar characteristics and meet the same needs from the point of view of the consumer" (*Commission v France (re Taxation of Spirits)* [1980]). If a product is judged to be "similar", then Article 90(1) applies (*John Walker v Ministeriet for Skatter* [1986]).

  If a product is not judged to be "similar", then Article 90(2) will come into play. This examines whether or not the products are likely to be in competition and assesses the protective effect of the disputed tax (*Commission v France (re Light Tobacco)* [2002]).

  Article 90 does not prohibit internal taxation. Member States are free to set up systems of taxation which they consider most appropriate for each product (*Commission v France (re Levy on Reprographic Machines)* [1981]). What it does prohibit is:

- Discrimination against imported products; and
- Indirect protection of domestic projects.

Not only taxation, but the method of assessment may be discriminatory. Two different systems of taxation, one applying to domestic products and another dealing with similar imported products cannot be justified (*Bobie v HZA Aachen-Nord* [1976]). In *Commission v Ireland* [1980] the tax was charged uniformly but whereas domestic producers were allowed several weeks' grace before payment was due, importers were faced with immediate payment upon importation.

Indirect Discrimination

While direct discriminatory taxation is easy to recognise in the light of the strict prohibition in Article 90, indirect discrimination is less easy to detect. In *Humblot v Directeur des Services Fiscaux* [1985], French road tax applied tax on cars above 16cv at 5,000 FF. It was established that France did not produce any cars with an engine size of more than 16cv so the disproportionately heavy tax affected only imported goods.

Objective Justification

Even if a Member State establishes a tax system based on factors which indirectly affect imports more drastically than domestic products, the Court will allow a Member State to plead that there was some objective policy reason acceptable to the Community as a whole to justify its action. In this way, the Treaty rules are prevented from becoming too harsh. These reasons may refer to the use of raw materials, the processes employed in the production of goods or general objectives of economic policy of a Member State such as protection of the environment or development of regional policy. In the case of *Commission v France* [1987], sweet wines made in the traditional manner tended to be produced in areas of poor soil and low rainfall and where the local economy was particularly dependent on wine output. It was therefore held to be objectively justifiable to give tax concessions in order to support economically weak regions. So although there was indirect discrimination, it was excusable for France to use its tax system as a way of strengthening regional economies—provided that the concession was kept open to all products, not only to domestically produced goods.

Similarly in *Commission v Italy* in 1980, Italy imposed a tax on imported and domestic cars based on their capacity to pollute which was objectively justified on the grounds of environmental protection although in the circumstances, it imposed a heavier tax burden on imported cars than on domestic cars.

However, in the 1997 case of *Commission v Greece* concerning a Greek rule providing for a reduced rate of tax to apply to cars using 'anti-pollution' technology which was not open to imports because of the practicalities of testing imported vehicles, the Court ruled that even consideration for the environment could not justify such discriminatory taxation.

The Relationship Between Article 25 (Customs Charges) and Article 90 (Discriminatory Taxation)

Both Articles are complementary, yet mutually exclusive. A charge may not be examined under Articles 25 and 90 at the same time.

In principle, if a charge is imposed exclusively on imported products, it is likely to be a charge equivalent to a customs duty. If a charge is levied on both domestic and imported products in a uniform manner, it is more likely to be part of a system of internal taxation. In *Firma Steinike und Weinlig v Bundesamt für Ernährung und Fortwirtschaft* [1977], the Court held that "financial charges within a general system of internal taxation applying systematically to domestic and imported products according to the same criteria are not to be considered charges having equivalent effect".

In order to distinguish which of the two provisions a charge is likely to fall under the Court has applied a test based on the destination of the proceeds of the charge. The case of *Fratelli Cucchi v Avez* in 1977, concerned a tax imposed on the sale of domestic and imported sugar. The proceeds of the tax provided subsidies for both Italian sugar refineries and for sugar beet producers. The Court concluded that a charge, which appeared to be part of a system of internal taxation, could be considered a charge having equivalent effect to a customs duty if the following conditions were met:

- The sole purpose of the charge must be to finance activities for the benefit of the taxed domestic product;
- The taxed product and the domestic product benefiting from the charge must be the same; and
- Any charges imposed on domestic products are made good in full.

These conditions are very strict. If all three exist, then it is a charge having equivalent effect to a customs duty prohibited under Article 25 and not part of a general system of taxation which might, if it is discriminatory be prohibited under Article 90. In both cases, unlawful charges must be repaid by the Member State.

Enforcing the Rules
Since Articles 23, 25 and 90 are directly effective, Member States may be called upon in national courts to repay any customs duties or other charges which have been found to be illegal (*Amministrazione delle Finanze dello Stato v San Giorgio* [1983]). Delictual liability may also arise with regard to breaches of Articles 25 and 90 by reason of the restrictive effect of a charge on imports from other Member States (*Just v Danish Ministry for Fiscal Affairs* [1980]).

QUANTITATIVE RESTRICTIONS AND MEASURES HAVING EQUIVALENT EFFECT TO QUANTITATIVE RESTRICTIONS

Abolishing charges on goods passing between Member States could not in themselves ensure that goods moved freely through the Community. Member States began to put up invisible barriers to trade which were not easily recognisable and as such were a more serious threat to the free movement of goods. Such measures were also capable of restricting the free movement of goods to a greater extent than charges.

A Member State may infringe these rules by failing to act as well as by acting. In *Commission v France* [1997], the Commission took action against France for failing to take all necessary and proportionate measures to prevent the free movement of fruit and vegetables from being obstructed by the actions of private individuals. Lorries transporting goods were intercepted, their loads destroyed and drivers threatened and attacked.

Contrast this with *Eugen Schmidberger* [2003] however where a peaceful protest on the Brenner motorway completely closed it to traffic for 30 hours. An action was brought against Austria but in this case, having weighed up the interests involved (respect for the demonstrators' rights of freedom of expression and assembly under the European Convention on Human Rights as against the free movement of goods), the Court found that as the Austrian authorities had taken steps to minimise the disturbance, a fair balance had been struck as achievement of both objectives would not have been able to have been carried out by measures less restrictive to community trade.

Article 28 (ex Article 30) lays down the basic provision:

> "Quantitative restrictions on imports and all measures having equivalent effect shall be prohibited between Member States."

Article 29 (ex Article 31) prohibits quantitative restrictions and measures having equivalent effect to quantitative restrictions (MEQRs), on exports:

> "Quantitative restrictions on exports and all measures having equivalent effect shall be prohibited between Member States."

Article 30 (ex Article 36) provides for derogations; that the prohibitions in Articles 28 and 29 will not apply because of specific justifications. These derogations are allowed on several grounds so long as:

- They do not arbitrarily discriminate against goods from another Member State; and
- Or are a disguised restriction on trade between member states.

Article 28
Article 28 prohibits two types of activity:

- Quantitative restrictions
- Measures having an equivalent effect to quantitative restrictions

It prevents Member States from imposing a numerical limit on the imports of a certain product in an effort to protect their own products from competition from other Member States.

Although Article 28 is addressed to Member States and concerns measures taken by them, measures taken by any public body, whether legislative, executive or judicial as well as any semi-public body which affect trade between Member States are prohibited (*Apple and Pear Development Council v K J Lewis Ltd* [1983]).

What are Quantitative Restrictions?
These were defined in the case of *Geddo v Ente Nazionale Risi* [1973], as measures which amount to a "total or partial restraint on imports, exports or goods in transit". In other words, import bans, setting of quotas, and such like.

What about Measures having Equivalent Effect to Quantitative Restrictions?
These proved more difficult to define. After some pressure from Member States and the European Parliament the Commission issued Directive 70/50 to clarify the meaning and scope of "measures having equivalent effect". Section 2 of this Directive proved to be particularly valuable in setting out in a non-exhaustive list of what would be considered a "measure having equivalent effect to a quantitative restriction" with respect to national measures which apply specifically to, or affect only imported products. These are often referred to as distinctly applicable measures. Such discriminatory measures included:

- Setting minimum or maximum sale prices;
- Fixing less favourable prices for imports;
- Lowering the value of imports by increasing its costs;

- Setting conditions of payment for imports differing from those of domestic products;
- Specifying conditions for packaging, composition, identification, size, weight, etc., which would only apply to imports;
- Limiting publicity for imports compared to domestic goods; and
- Making it mandatory for importers to have an agent in the importing state.

The Directive also refers to measures which are non-discriminatory or *indistinctly applicable*, that is, applying to both imports and exports but which may nevertheless restrict trade from abroad by, for example, setting disproportionately restrictive requirements on importers. The Court has developed its caselaw on many of these cases where it has established that the same objective can be attained by other, less burdensome means.

In *Procureur du Roi v Dassonville* [1974], the Court set out its own definition of "measures having equivalent effect" and addressed the double burden an importer may have to bear in that having already complied with domestic laws, he may also have to change his method of production or documentation to comply with the importing state's laws. Dassonville had imported a consignment of Scotch whisky to Belgium from France, without the certificate of origin required by Belgian law. This certificate proved impossible to produce and Dassonville went ahead with the transaction. The company was charged under Belgian law with the criminal offence of importing goods without the requisite certificate of origin and argued that this contravened Article 28.

The Court stated what has become known as "the *Dassonville* formula",

> "all trading rules enacted by member states which are capable of hindering directly or indirectly, actually or potentially, intra-Community trade, are to be considered as measures having an effect equivalent to quantitative restrictions."

This definition includes both distinctly applicable measures affecting imports and indistinctly applicable measures affecting imports and domestic products. More importantly, the judgment emphasises the effect of the restrictive practice, not the form it takes. The objectionable part of the Belgian law was that its effect hindered the free movement of goods. The Court continued,

> "in the absence of a Community system guaranteeing for consumers the authenticity of a product's designation of origin, if a member state takes measures to prevent unfair practices .... *those measures should be reasonable* and the means of proof required should not act as a hindrance to trade between member states [emphasis added]."

The *Dassonville* case was fundamental in dismantling many of the obstacles by which Member States were endeavouring to discriminate against imports and protect their own products in the process of which they were infringing Community law.

A similar but more recent case involving labelling was that of *Commission v Spain and Italy* [2003]. The Court held that the requirement in those countries to alter the sales name of chocolate made according to Directive 73/241 in Denmark, Ireland, Portugal, Sweden, Finland and the UK was disproportionate and infringed the principle of the free movement of goods. Appropriate labelling would have been sufficient to ensure that consumers were informed and thus protected.

In *Commission v Ireland* [1982], the Irish Goods Council conducted a campaign to promote Irish products. The Court held that the campaign was in breach of Article 28 as it intended to substitute domestic products for imports in the Irish market the effect of which would be to restrict imports from other Member States.

Not all measures which promote domestic goods will be caught by Article 28. In *Apple and Pear Development Council* [1983], although this body was set up by the UK Government, it was financed by fees paid by domestic growers and its task was to promote the consumption of apples and pears. It brought actions against some of the fruit growers who refused to pay the charge. The actions were defended on the basis that the charges were contrary to Article 28. In its judgment, the Court stated that a Member State would be entitled to promote its own products, but that the marketing in question would be considered unlawful under Article 28 if it was intended to discourage the purchase of imported products. Competition in terms of quality is desirable, but discrimination on the grounds of nationality infringes Community law.

In *Commission v Italy* [1991], Italian public authorities had to buy Italian made cars before they could get subsidies. This measure discriminated against imports, affected trade between Member States and was thus prohibited.

In *Tasca* [1976], Tasca attempted to sell sugar above the maximum price set by the Italian authorities for both imported and domestic sugar. While national law prohibiting price increases on sugar would not of itself constitute a measure having equivalent effect (indistinctly applicable), if prices are fixed at such a low level that the sale of imports becomes more difficult or costly than the sale of domestic sugar, then the Member State would be in breach of Community law.

In *Openbaar Ministerie v Van Tiggele* [1978], criminal proceedings were brought against Van Tiggele for selling gin below the national fixed price. The fixing of a minimum price for both imported and domestic products was not in breach of Article 28, provided it did not restrict imports. However, it would be unlawful if importers were to be placed at a relative disadvantage because they could not make any profit on their products under these circumstances or because the competitive advantage conferred by lower prices is cancelled out. The Dutch law was in breach of Article 28.

After *Dassonville*, the next major development was the case of *Cassis de Dijon (Rewe-Zentral AG v Bundermonopolverwaltung für Branntwein)* in 1979. German law laid down a minimum alcohol content of 25 per cent for cassis—a blackcurrant liqueur—though the alcohol content of the French cassis was only 15 per cent. Although this minimum level applied both to imports and domestic goods, its effect was to exclude French cassis from the German market. This measure was challenged by German importers on the grounds that it infringed Article 28.

What emerges from the *Cassis* case are two fundamental principles of Community law. The first is the "rule of reason", whereby if there is no Community legislation on a particular topic, each Member State is free to take reasonable measures to prevent unfair trade practices. Prior to *Cassis* the emphasis had been on whether or not the measure had been discriminatory; now the rule of reason sets out a non-exhaustive list of the type of measures a Member State may take, though these must be proportionate.

The second *Cassis* principle is that of mutual recognition. It states that if goods have been lawfully produced and marketed in one Member State, complying with the mandatory requirements of that State, there should be no valid reason why they should not be imported into any other Member State.

This judgment in *Cassis* built upon the foundations of *Dassonville* and meant that:

- In the absence of Community rules regarding the production and marketing of goods each Member State is free to lay down its own rules;
- Which must be in proportion to the measure taken;
- But not if these rules have the effect of hindering intra-Community trade;
- And only if these rules were mandatory—to defend consumers, protect public health, promote fair trade and the effectiveness of fiscal supervision; and
- If the goods are lawfully produced and marketed in one Member State there must be clearly justifiable reasons why they cannot be sold in another Member State.

Cassis was also important because it removed the assumption after Dassonville that Article 28 would only apply where discrimination between imports and domestic products could be shown.

In *Oosthoek's* [1982], national law restricted the distribution of free gifts in the interests of consumers. The Court stated that

"the possibility cannot be ruled out that to compel a producer either to adopt advertising or sales promotion schemes which differ from one Member State to another or to discontinue a scheme which he considers to be particularly effective may constitute an obstacle to imports even if the legislation in question applies to domestic products and imported products without distinction."

In *Walter Rau Lebensmittelwerke v De Smedt PVBA* [1987], the Court ruled that a Belgian requirement that margarine should be sold in cube-shaped boxes in order to distinguish it from butter was disproportionate. Consumers would be sufficiently protected by appropriate and clear labelling of the product than such a method which would be likely to hinder intra-Community trade.

In *Commission v Germany (re German Beer Purity Laws)* [1987], the Court held that German law stating that the word "bier" could only be used for products brewed in accordance with the country's special laws on brewing were disproportionate in that they went far beyond what was necessary to protect public health, the ostensible reason for the German legislation.

In *Cinéthèque* [1985], French law prohibited the marketing of videos of films, both domestic and imported, during the first year of the film's release. The Court stated that although the protection of cultural activities constituted a mandatory requirement, this particular requirement would create a barrier to trade in videos between Member States.

In *Commission v United Kingdom (re Origin Marking of Retail Goods)* [1985], the Court stated that a UK requirement to protect consumers by marking all goods with their country of origin would affect trade between Member States as such marking might encourage consumers to exercise their prejudices in favour of national products and avoid Community-produced goods.

In *Commission v Denmark (re Returnable Containers)* [1989], the Court held that despite special arrangements for importers as an exception to the Danish requirement for approved reusable containers, this national rule was disproportionate. The concession for limited quantities of imports was not sufficient to redeem the breach of Article 28.

On October 3, 1980, the Commission adopted a Communication concerning the consequences of the *Cassis* judgment ([1980] O.J. C256/2). It read as follows:

"Any product imported from another Member State must in principle be admitted to the territory of the importing State if it has been lawfully produced, that is, conforms to rules and processes of manufacturer that are customary and traditionally accepted in the exporting country, and is marketed in the territory of another."

Nevertheless, some cases relating to the retail sector illustrate the difficulties encountered in ascertaining whether or not a measure fell within Article 28.

In *Torfaen B.C. v B & Q plc* [1989], a retail superstore was prosecuted for violation of the Sunday Trading Act of 1950 which had the effect of reducing sales by about 10 per cent with a corresponding reduction in imports from other Member States. B & Q claimed this constituted a "measure having equivalent effect" within Article 28. After some confusion as to what constituted a "trading rule" it was held that such measures were a "legitimate part of economic and social policy" and were designed to accord with "national or regional socio-cultural characteristics". The Court held that English Sunday trading rules did not, therefore breach Article 28 provided that their restrictive effect was not disproportionate to their purpose.

In *Ministère Publique v Marchandise* [1989], a Belgian law which prohibited the employment of workers in shops on Sunday after noon was held not to be disproportionate to the socio-cultural aim pursued.

In *Stoke on Trent City Council v B & Q plc* [1992], the question of English Sunday trading rules again came before the Court. It ruled that the Sunday Trading Act was within the prohibition set out in Article 28 but that it could be allowed to stand provided its objective was justified under Community law and in proportion to the aim to be achieved.

However, the Court in *Keck and Mithouard* [1993], the Court decided to "re-examine and clarify" its caselaw. Keck and Mithouard were convicted of selling goods at a loss contrary to French law. The Court stated the *Dassonville* formula did not apply to selling arrangements if "the provisions apply to all affected traders operating within the national territory and provided that they affect in the same manner, in law and in fact, the marketing of domestic products and those from other Member States".

Member States could thus determine their own measures to regulate selling arrangements where these would have no effect on imports and would not discriminate against imported goods. They would not fall within the prohibition of Article 28.

Although challenges to national measures allegedly infringing Article 28 continued to be made, the Court dismissed them. These included:

- *Groupement National des Negociants en Pommes de Terre de Belgique (Belgapom) v ITM Belgium SA and Vocarex SA* [1995], concerned resale of potatoes at a loss. Vocarex argued that the Belgian law prohibiting this practice was prohibited under Article 28. The Court considered that this fell under selling arrangements;

- *Hünermund v Landesapothekerkammer Baden-Württemburg* [1993], German rules prohibiting certain advertising by pharmacists were also considered as selling arrangements, thus falling outside Article 28;

- *Tankstation 'T Heukske and Boermans* [1994], Dutch restrictions on the closing opening hours of petrol stations did not fall within Article 28.

While not all national rules which might hinder trade between Member States can be classified as selling arrangements, rather than rules which relate to the intrinsic characteristics of the goods themselves, it seems that *Keck* has clarified the law so that measures will constitute selling arrangements "so long as they apply to all relevant traders operating within the Member State and so long as they affect in the same manner, in law and in fact, the marketing of domestic products and those from other Member States".

Exports—Article 29
Article 29 reads:

"Quantitative restrictions on exports, and all measures having equivalent effect, shall be prohibited between Member States."

So far most of the cases considered have involved national measures on imports. Article 29 applies in much the same way as Article 28 but it refers to *exports*. The principle of a Member State's action in hindering Community trade is the same.

In *Procureur de la République Besançon v Bouhelier* [1977], a French law which necessitated quality checks on watches for exports, but no checks on watches which were to be sold in France was held to be a measure equivalent to a quantitative restriction on exports.

In *PB Groenveld* [1979], a Dutch law prohibited all domestic producers of meat products from stocking or processing horsemeat. This would avoid the risk of exporting horsemeat to countries which did not allow its sale. The Court stated that:

"national measures which have as their specific object or effect the restriction of patterns of exports and thereby the establishment of a difference in treatment between the domestic trade of a Member State and its export trade in such a way as to provide a particular advantage for national production or for the domestic market of the State in question at the expense of the production or of trade of other Member States."

Derogations

Article 30 (ex Article 36) provides for exceptions to the fundamental rule that all obstacles to the free movement of goods between Member States should be abolished. The Court has stated that like all derogations, this list of exceptions should be interpreted strictly. It will scrutinise national rules which discriminate against goods from other Member States before it confirms a derogation. It will not extend the derogations beyond those listed in Article 30. The list is exhaustive.

Article 30 reads as follows:

"The provisions of Articles 28 and 29 shall not preclude prohibitions or restrictions on imports, exports or goods in transit justified on grounds of public morality, public policy or public security; the protection of health and life of human, animals or plants; the protection of national treasures possessing artistic, historic or archaeological value; or the protection of industrial and commercial property. Such prohibitions or restrictions shall not however, constitute a means of arbitrary discrimination or a disguised restriction on trade between Member States."

Article 30 is in two parts. The first part lists the exceptions to the prohibitions. The second part goes on to warn Member States that any derogation submitted must not be a means of arbitrary discrimination or a disguised restriction on intra-Community trade.

When a Member State claims that the measure at issue has been adopted under one of these derogations, it must establish:

* That it is necessary for the measure to be adopted—the test of necessity; and
* That the measure chosen was the least restrictive means of achieving the objective—the test of proportionality.

Arbitrary discrimination means that the measure gives advantages to the marketing of domestic products—or imports—or exports from one Member State at the expense of another (*Commission v France (re Advertising of Alcoholic Beverages)* [1980]).

Disguised restrictions are measures which are ostensibly justified under Article 30, but which have the effect of restricting the free movement of goods (*Commission v UK (re Imports of Poultry Meat)* [1982]).

Where the Community has already taken action to make sure that there are harmonising measures or standards set up in a particular area, Member States may not justify their own national rules which infringe Article 28 and restrict intra-community trade, by pleading exemption through Article 30.

The burden of proof rests upon the Member State relying on the derogation.

Public Morality

Member States may set out what constitutes public morality in accordance with their own scales of values. However, they must not impose double standards—one to prevent the sale and marketing of domestic products and another relating only to imports.

In *R v Henn and Darby* in 1979, the defendants were charged with importing "indecent or obscene articles" into the UK from the Netherlands. They pleaded that this UK law was contrary to the free movement of goods despite the UK government's assertion that the prohibition on such imports fell within the derogation on "public morality". On the other hand in the case of *Conegate* [1986], the seizure of similar material was not justified under Article 30. On this occasion, the Court stated that because it was legal to manufacture the material in the UK—although it was subject to restrictions on where and to whom it might be sold—the UK itself was not in a position to restrict similar imports from abroad.

Public Policy

Under this heading a Member State must show the imports or exports in question would be a genuine and sufficiently serious threat to one of the fundamental interests of its society. In *Thompson* [1978], criminal proceedings were commenced against UK citizens who imported gold coins despite a ban on such activity. The UK's submission succeeded on the grounds of public policy.

The Court has ruled on all other cases very strictly. What has been ruled to be inapplicable to the public policy derogation are measures that seek to excuse Member State action on the grounds of:

- Avoidance of civil unrest which the national authorities were well able to cope with—*Cullet v Centre Leclerc* [1985];
- Restriction of criminal behaviour—*Prantl* [1984]; and
- Protection of consumers—*Kohl v Ringelhan* [1984].

Public Security

In *Campus Oil Ltd v Minister for Industry and Energy* [1984], the Irish government succeeded before the Court with its requirement that importers buy one-third of what they needed from the State-owned oil refinery on the grounds that without this revenue, the refinery would have to close down. This would mean that Ireland would have no source of oil to supply key national institutions and services in the event of a national crisis.

Protection of the Health and Life of Humans, Animals and Plants

The Court considers that the "health and life of humans ranks first among the interests protected" by Article 30 (*De Peijper* [1975]). In *Commission v UK (re UHT Milk)* [1983], the Court accepted a justification that an import licence system was necessary to regulate the heat treatment of imported milk and to trace the origins of infected milk, but re-treating and re-packaging imported milk was an unjustified restriction on trade because milk from other Member States was already subject to similar controls before export. This requirement was simply a disguised restriction on intra-Community trade.

In *R v Royal Pharmaceutical Society ex parte API* [1989], the code of ethics laid down by the pharmacists' professional body did not allow a pharmacist to substitute, except in an emergency, any other medicine for that specifically named in a doctor's prescription, even where the pharmacist believed that the effect and quality of the substitute were identical. The Court found this rule discriminated against imports but accepted the UK's justification as being on the grounds of public health.

The protection of the health and life of animals was successfully pleaded until Article 30 in *Bluhme* [1998], where in order to protect the Læsø brown bee, the Court ruled that a Danish law prohibiting the importation of other live bees on to the island of Læsø was illegal.

Protection of National Treasures Possessing Artistic, Historic or Archaeological Value

Member States are entitled to determine the value of their national treasures possessing artistic, historic or archaeological value and may determine restrictions on their import. However, any protection afforded may not justify charges (*Commission v Italy (First Art Treasures Case)* [1968]).

In the mid-1990s, legislation was adopted to ensure that the free movement of goods would not increase illegal exports of such national treasures (Directive 93/7 on the Return of Cultural Objects Unlawfully Removed from the Territory of a Member State and Regulation 3911/92 on the Control of the Export of Cultural Goods).

---

10. FREE MOVEMENT OF WORKERS

The free movement of workers constitutes one of the cornerstones of the internal market. An extensive system of Treaty provisions, secondary legislation and the caselaw of the Court has provided for a system of employment rights throughout the Community prohibiting national legislation which might place other Community nationals at a disadvantage when they seek to exercise their right of free movement. The basic principle covering these rights is that of non-discrimination of persons from other Member States on the grounds of nationality as set out in Article 12 (ex Article 6). This principle is incorporated within all the other provisions in this area either through the Treaty, in the secondary legislation or through the caselaw of the Court.

Among the provisions promoting free movement of workers are the following:

- Article 17 (ex Article 8) establishes citizenship of the European Union. Every person holding the nationality of a Member State is a citizen of the Union. Citizenship of the Union complements and does not replace national citizenship. Under Article 18, (ex Article 8a) every Union citizen has the right to move and reside freely within the territory of the Member States, subject to the limitations and conditions laid down in the

Treaty and by the secondary legislation adopted to give effect to these provisions.

- Article 39 (ex Article 48) defines what is meant by free movement of workers. This is considered in detail below.
- Article 40 (ex Article 49) relates to the implementation of Article 39 by setting out the legislative manner in which the goal of free movement may be achieved. It relates to close co-operation between national employment services, abolishing restrictions and by setting up appropriate machinery "to match offers of employment into touch with applications for employment and to facilitate the achievement of a balance between supply and demand in the employment market in such a way as to avoid serious threats to the standard of living and level of employment in the various regions and industries".
- Article 41 (ex Article 50) provides for the exchange of young workers.
- Article 42 (ex Article 51) relates to social security in relation to the free movement of workers.
- Article 12 (ex Article 6) provides a general prohibition of discrimination on the grounds of nationality.
- The Treaty of Amsterdam introduced a new Article 13 to promote action to combat discrimination based on sex, racial or ethnic origin, religion or belief, disability, age or sexual orientation (*see also* Chapter 13, Equal Pay and Treatment).

Several major pieces of secondary legislation also facilitate those falling within their personal scope to exercise their right of free movement. These are as follows:

- **Regulation 1612/68** (amended in July 1990) on access to, and conditions of employment.
- **Directive 1251/70** on the right to remain in the territory of a host Member State after having been employed there.
- **Directive 68/360** on the right of entry and residence, complements Regulation 1612/68 by requiring the abolition of restrictions on the movement and residence of nationals of the Member States and their families to whom Regulation 1612/68 applies. Member States must issue or renew identity cards or passports to such persons. They must be allowed to enter a host Member State simply by producing a valid identity card/passport. No entry visa may be demanded except for those members of the worker's family who are not nationals of any Member State (*R v Pieck* [1980]).
- **Directive 64/221** on the right of Member States to derogate from the provisions of the Treaty on the grounds of public policy, public security and public health.

Article 39 (ex Article 48) sets out that:

"(1) Freedom of movement for workers shall be secured within the Community.

(2) Such freedom of movement shall entail the abolition of any discrimination based on nationality between workers of the Member States as regards employment, remuneration and other conditions of work and employment.

(3) It shall entail the rights, subject to limitations justified on grounds of public policy, public security or public health—
(a) to accept offers of employment actually made;
(b) to move freely within the territory of Member States for this purpose;
(c) to stay in a Member State for the purpose of employment in accordance with this provisions governing the employment of nationals of that State laid down by law, regulation or administrative action;
to remain in the territory of a Member State after having been employed in that State, subject to conditions which shall be embodied in implementing regulations to be drawn up by the Commission.
(4) The provisions of this Article shall not apply to employment in the public sector."

Article 39 is directly effective (*Royer* [1977]), both vertically against a Member State and horizontally, against employers (*Clean Car Autoservice* [1998]).

Free movement and its associated Community rights are not unconditional. Some restrictions apply:

- A worker must exercise his Community right to free movement in order to benefit from employment rights in another Member State. Community rights do not apply if a worker moves from one region of his home country to another. In such cases, the relevant national law applies (*R v Saunders* [1979] and *Morson and Jhabjan* [1982]).
- Member States may also restrict access to employment of other Member State nationals on the grounds of public policy, public security and public health (Article 39(3) and Directive 64/221).
- Member States may reserve access to employment in the public service to their own nationals under certain conditions (Article 39(4)).

The Community protection afforded also applies to those who move from one Member State to another to seek work. In *R v IAT ex parte Antonissen* in 1991, a Belgian national had entered the UK but more than six months later he had still not succeeded in finding a job. The Court said that deportation would be allowed where an individual had been in a member state for more than six months, unless he could produce evidence that he was still seeking work and had a genuine chance of being offered employment.

All the rights under Article 39 and its associated secondary legislation are granted to workers and their families. The families' rights depend on their relationships with the worker.

WHAT IS A WORKER?

Neither Article 39 nor the secondary legislation defines the term "worker". In clarifying its scope the Court has emphasised that "worker" must have a Community meaning inasmuch as it defines the scope of one of the fundamental freedoms of the Community. It must thus be interpreted widely (*Bettray v Staatssecretaris van Justitie* [1989]). In this and in other cases, the

Court further interpreted the term "worker". The criteria for qualifying as a worker within the meaning of Article 39 are that a person performs services of some economic value for and under the direction of another person, in return for which he/she receives remuneration (*Lawrie Blum* [1986]).

- *Hoekstra v BBDA* [1964], although having lost her job in the Netherlands Mrs Hoekstra was capable of taking another. The Court ruled that the term "worker" applied not exclusively to one who is currently employed but to a person "who is likely to remain in the territory of a Member State after having been employed in that state".
- *Levin* [1982], Mrs Levin was a part-time chambermaid working for wages below the minimum subsistence considered necessary in the Netherlands. As long as the work met the economic activity criterion, it did not matter whether or not the individual could support themselves on the money they earned.
- *Lawrie-Blum* [1986], Miss Lawrie-Blum was a trainee teacher working under supervision but receiving remuneration for conducting classes.
- *Kempf* [1986], Mr Kempf was a part-time music teacher who gave lessons for twelve hours a week. The Court stated that it did not matter whether the money used to supplement the income was from the individual's private means or from public funds.
- *Steymann* [1988], Mr Steymann was a member of a religious commune who undertook plumbing and general household duties for board, lodgings and pocket money but not a formal wage. The outside work which he also undertook—a necessary part of the commune's self-sufficiency—was held to be a genuine and effective economic activity.
- *URSAFF v Hostellerie le Manoir* [1991], the term "worker" was held to cover students on courses which required practical work experience in another Member State.
- *Raulin* [1992], the concept of "a worker" included a person who worked occasionally under a contract with no fixed hours but according to the needs of an employer.
- *CPM Meeusen v Hoofddirectie Van De Informatie Beheer Groep* [1999], a person related by marriage to the director and sole shareholder of the company may be classified as a "worker" if he/she pursues an effective and genuine economic activity.

But in *Bettray* the Court refused to accept that an individual who was working in a drug rehabilitation scheme was in fact a worker, because no real and genuine economic activity was taking place.

The Court has continued to abide by the three-part Community definition of a worker as set out in *Lawrie-Blum* (above). This is that the individual concerned:

- Performs a service of economic value;
- For and under the direction of another person; and
- Receives payment.

REGULATION 1612/68

This major piece of secondary legislation provides that any national of a Member State, irrespective of his residence, has the right to take up activity as an employed person and to pursue this activity within the territory of another Member State in accordance with the provisions laid down governing the employment of nationals of that Member State. In particular, he must have the right to take up any available employment in the host Member State under the same conditions as those allowed to nationals of that State. His spouse and children who are under the age of 21 or dependent on him, have the right to take up any employment throughout the territory of that same State even if they are not nationals of any Member State of the Union. In addition, dependent relatives in the ascending line of the worker and his spouse, have the right to live with the worker. The worker is entitled to all the housing rights and benefits accorded to national workers. His children are entitled to be admitted to general education, apprenticeship and vocational training courses under the same conditions as nationals of the host Member State. The worker is entitled to the same social and tax advantages and access to the same training in vocational schools and retraining centres as a national worker. Any collective or individual agreement regarding eligibility for employment, remuneration and other conditions of work or dismissal is null and void to the extent that it discriminates against workers who are nationals of another Member State.

This Regulation therefore gives valuable rights to workers, in particular concerning:

- Eligibility *for employment*;
- Equality of treatment *within employment*; and
- Rights for the families of those who *are employed*.

The material scope of the main sections of the Regulation are set out below.

Eligibility for Employment
Articles 1 to 6 of the Regulation allow migrant workers from another Member State the right to take up employment under the same conditions as the host State's nationals. This means that Member States must not specify discriminatory employment policies and companies must not operate such practices. In particular, they cannot discriminate in methods of recruitment, advertising vacancies or setting eligibility standards to apply for employment. However, Article 3(1) allows Member States to impose conditions "relating to linguistic knowledge required by reason of the nature of the post to be filled" (*Groener* [1989]). Article 4 prohibits quota systems setting out what percentage of foreign nationals may be employed (*Commission v France (Re French Merchant Seamen)* [1974]) and *Bosman* [1995]. Article 5 requires that similar assistance must be extended to nationals of other Member States in finding employment as is given to national workers.

Equality of Treatment Within Employment
Article 7(1) of the Regulation provides that workers from another Member State must not be treated differently from national workers—especially

regarding payment of wages or salary, dismissal and reinstatement, or re-employment if he/she becomes unemployed. Any discriminatory practices will be prohibited unless they can be justified under Article 39(4) of the Treaty (*Schöning-Kougebetopoulou v Freie und Hansestadt Hamburg* [1998]).

Social and Tax Advantages

Article 7(2) of the Regulation lays down that there should be no discrimination in social and tax advantages for workers. This covers matters such as a lower separation allowance for workers from another Member State and includes public service workers (*Sotgiu v Deutsche Bundespost* [1974]). This prohibition on discrimination applies even when these advantages are not related to a contract of employment—such as a war pension in *Even* [1979] and may remain even if the worker dies so that his family can benefit—such as concessionary cards for rail travel (*Cristini* [1975]). It does not cover social security benefits to which migrant workers are entitled only if they contribute to a social security scheme in a host Member State (*Frilli v Belgium* [1972]).

- In *Reina* [1982], migrant workers were held to be entitled to a special discretionary childbirth loan which was until then payable only to German nationals.
- In *Castelli* [1984], a payment made to all old people in Belgium but not to an Italian widow living with her retired son in Belgium was also considered unlawful.
- In *Bernini* [1992], a study grant was allowed to a dependent child of a migrant worker under the same conditions as those applicable to children of national workers.
- In *Scrivner* [1985], a minimum income allowance was allowed to members of the family of an unemployed worker.
- In *Commission v Luxembourg* [2002], a Luxembourg law providing for a guaranteed minimum income, but paid only to individuals who had lived in Luxembourg for at least 5 of the previous 20 years before application was held to be indirectly discriminatory against nationals of other Member States.

Vocational Training

Article 7(3) of the Regulation concerns vocational training. In *Brown v Secretary of State for Scotland* [1988], the applicant had obtained sponsorship from a UK company prior to taking up a university place. He then applied for a grant which was refused. The Court found that the course was not "vocational training" within the meaning of Article 7(3) though it would constitute a social and tax advantage under Article 7(2). This in turn was only available to workers fulfilling the criteria in *Lawrie-Blum*. The Court decided that Brown was not entitled to a grant despite his status of a worker because he "acquired that status exclusively as a result of his being accepted for admission to undertake the studies in question".

However, in *Lair* [1988], the applicant was a French national who had worked in Germany for five years and had requested a similar grant from the German government. Again this was held not to be vocational training under

Article 7(3) but because she had been a worker, she was entitled to social and tax advantages under Article 7(2) even if she was involuntarily unemployed. However, the Court stated that a migrant worker who gave up a job to pursue further training would only be eligible for a grant when there was a close link between the work and the subject studied.

Workers' Families

Article 10(1) of the Regulation defines what is means by "members of a worker's family" for the purpose of deciding who will be allowed to migrate with the worker to the host State. These are:

- A worker's spouse and descendants who are under the age of 21 or are dependants; and
- Dependant relatives in the ascending line of the worker and his spouse.

In the case of *Lebon* [1987], it was established that even if an adult child is over 21, if he or she is still dependant, then they are still regarded in law as members of the family and are entitled to claim Community family rights. The dependency is as a result of a factual situation, not derived from the national legislation of a host Member State.

The Court has made clear in the case of *Reed* [1986], that "spouse" only means an individual married to the worker though because of the principle of non-discrimination, a Member State cannot refuse a cohabitee of a national of another Member State if the host Member State's law provide this right for its own nationals. If a married couple separates at any time, spouse's rights do not come to an end until they are divorced (*Diatta* [1985]).

Members of a worker's family are entitled to migrate with the worker regardless of their own nationality—though of course the worker must be the national of another Member State. Family rights under Regulation 1612/68 are entirely dependent on the worker who must have exercised his/her right to cross-border movement (*Morson and Jhabjan v the Netherlands* [1982]).

Article 12 provides that children are entitled to non-discriminatory access not only to general educational, apprenticeship and vocational training courses but also grants and loans (*Casagrande* [1974]).

Other rights for migrant workers which confer equal treatment with nationals contained in Regulation 1612/68 include Trade Union Rights (Article 8) and Housing (Article 9).

REGULATION 1251/70

This Regulation extends the right to remain in a Member State after having been employed in that Member State to:

- Retired workers;
- Workers who are permanently incapacitated and unable to work; and
- Frontier workers.

Three conditions relating to length of time of work and residence allow the right to remain permanently in the host Member State. These are contained in Article 2(1) of the Regulation:

(1) (With regard to retired workers.) The worker has worked in the host Member State for the last 12 months, lived there for the previous three years and has now retired.

(2) (With regard to incapacitated workers.) The worker has lived in the host member state for the previous two years and has stopped working because of permanent incapacity.

(3) (With regard to trans-frontier workers.) The worker has lived and worked in the Host State for three years, but takes a job in another Member State while continuing to live in the first Member State.

In all cases, the worker's family is allowed to stay permanently, even after the worker dies. And the family is also entitled to equal treatment as in Regulation 1612/68 including social and tax advantages.

DIRECTIVE 68/360

The right of entry to and residence in another Member State other than one's own in order to look for work, pursue an activity as an employed or self-employed person is conferred directly by the Treaty in Articles 39 and 43. Directive 68/360 elaborates on these rights. It also recognises that certain formalities must be complied with, though these are reduced to a minimum. These rights are not dependent on the host Member State:

- Workers have the right to leave their home country to look for work elsewhere (Article 2 of the Directive) by being issued with a passport or valid identity card.
- To enter another Member State the worker only needs to produce a valid identity card though the host Member State may require an entry visa for family members who are not Community nationals (Article 3(2)).
- To obtain a residence permit, the worker must produce a valid passport/identity card plus a confirmation of employment within the host Member State. Family members of a worker must produce their documents of entry and a document issued by the competent authorities of their home Member State proving their relationship with the worker. If they are dependent on the worker they are required to submit a document issued by the same authorities certifying that they are dependent on the worker or that they lived with him in that country (Article 4(3)(c), (d) and (e)). The residence permit must be valid throughout the host Member State for at least five years and renewable automatically—unless it is a temporary job or the worker becomes involuntarily unemployed.

A failure to comply with formalities regarding entry and residence cannot justify a deportation order. Any such sanctions must be subject to the principle of proportionality (*Watson and Belmann* [1976]).

EXCEPTIONS TO THE FREE MOVEMENT OF WORKERS
Article 39(3) and Directive 64/221

As well as requiring a worker to *exercise* the right to free movement between Member States before claiming the benefit of Community rights, exceptions allowing a Member State to restrict this right arise with the derogations set out in Article 39(3) in conjunction with Directive 64/221. These derogations are limited to only three; public policy, public security and public health. The Directive also covers the issue or renewal of residence permits, expulsion from the territory of a host Member State and sets out procedural safeguards which must be followed by public authorities if they seek to exclude non-nationals.

In view of an increasing number of complaints from citizens concerning problems arising from restrictions on free movement, the Commission adopted a Communication in July 1999. It aimed to improve implementation of citizens' rights by reducing differences between Member States' interpretation of the rules and by raising citizens' awareness of their rights. In this, the Commission took account of the concept of Union citizenship and paid particular attention to the caselaw of the Court.

The derogations under Article 39(3) only apply when a Member State considers the exclusion of an individual from its territory, but they cannot be used to discriminate against him regarding his employment once the individual has lawfully entered the country.

Public Policy and Public Security

These derogations must be:

- Interpreted strictly (*Van Duyn* [1974]);
- Proportional to the objective pursued (*Bond Van Adverteerders* [1988]); and
- Based exclusively on the personal conduct of the person involved (Article 3(1) of the Directive). Previous criminal convictions are not in themselves sufficient grounds for taking any measures, such as deportation.

In *Bonsignore* [1975], an Italian working in Germany accidentally shot and killed his brother. This did not carry a prison sentence but Bonsignore was convicted of possession of a unlicensed gun and received a deportation order as a general preventative measure to deter other immigrants from committing similar offences. The Court stated that such measures must be based solely on the personal conduct of the person concerned.

In *Bouchereau* [1977], a Frenchman working in Britain was recommended for deportation after he had twice been convicted of drug offences. Again, the Court looked strictly at the UK's reasons for deportation and stated that the public policy derogation may only be invoked where there is a genuine, sufficiently serious and present threat to one of the fundamental interests of society.

In *Adoui and Cornuaille* [1982], two French prostitutes appealed against the Belgian authorities' refusal to grant then a residence permit, despite prostitution not being an offence in Belgium. The Court considered that Member States may only justify restrictions on the admission to, or residence within, its territory on nationals of another Member State if it adopted, with respect to the same conduct on the part of its own nationals, repressive measures or other genuine and effective measures intended to combat such conduct.

In *Mary Carpenter* [2002] a Philippine national married to a UK citizen faced deportation for outstaying her original leave to enter the country. The Court held that the decision to deport did not strike a fair balance between the competing interests of respect for family life and the maintenance of public order and public safety. Ms Carpenter's personal conduct had never been the subject of complaint, the marriage was genuine and in those circumstances, the Court considered that deporting her would be an infringement of a right that was not proportionate to the objective pursued.

Public Health
Derogation from the principles of free movement on the grounds of public health may only be invoked to refuse entry or residence for the first time, where the individual suffers from one of the infectious or contagious diseases listed in Group A of the Annex to Directive 64/221 or under Group B, diseases or disabilities which might public policy or public security, such as drug addition and profound mental disturbance. The development of a disease or disability after being admitted to the country on a valid residence permit does not justify a refusal to renew the permit, or allow deportation.

The Public Service Exception
Under Article 39(4), Member States may deny or restrict access to employment in the public services to nationals from other Member States. Because of the potential for Member States lawfully to extend preference to their own nationals and thereby discriminate against other Community nationals by classifying a wide variety of jobs as those within the public service, the Court stated that this exception should be interpreted strictly.

In *Sotgiu v Deutsche Bundespost* [1974], the Court said:

- Article 39(4) only applied to certain activities connected with the exercise of official authority.
- Since the employees concerned worked for branches of the government of the Member States, the legal designations of the jobs could be easily be varied by the Member States themselves. These designations should therefore be set by the Court to prevent discrimination against nationals from other Member States.
- Article 39(4) only applied to access to employment, not to conditions of work, once a person had been employed. If a person was sufficiently loyal or trustworthy to be admitted to such employment in the first place, there were no grounds for paying them less or treating them differently because of their nationality.

In *Commission v Belgium (No. 1)* [1980], the Court reiterated that like all derogations, the public service exception must be interpreted narrowly and uniformly, with a Community meaning. It continued "for a state to justify excluding non-nationals the post in question must require a special relationship of allegiance to the state and the reciprocity of rights and duties which formed the foundation of the bond of nationality."

The requirement for such posts to possess such allegiance and to depend upon the bond of nationality was two-fold:

(1) The posts must involve participation in the exercise of powers conferred by public law; and

(2) They must entail duties designed to safeguard the general interests of the State.

The approach taken was functional—the nature and character of the posts were important rather than their titles.

In 1988 the Commission published a document setting out some guidance on employment which it considered would not fall within the exception ([1988] O.J. C72/2). These covered posts in public health services, teaching in State schools, research for non-military purposes and public bodies responsible for administering commercial services. What would continue to be within the public service exception would be members of the armed forces, police and judiciary. There has obviously been tension in this area of law. Member States believe this is an area where a State should be able to exercise its full sovereignty and employ who they wish to serve the State without having to abide by Community rules of non-discrimination. The Commission has attempted to balance this understandable desire by setting out jobs which are security-sensitive as opposed to those which are not.

In *Scholz* [1994], it was stated that "public service would be taken into account" for Ms Scholz's application for canteen work in Italy. Although she relied on her previous experience in the German public sector, the Italian authorities stated that this must be public service in Italy. This discrimination was held to be unlawful as the job itself did not warrant it.

In the case of *Colgan (Katherine)* [1997], restrictions imposed on entry to the Civil Service in Northern Ireland as a management trainee were held to be illegal, disproportionate and not justified by Article 39(4).

Procedural Safeguards
Directive 64/221 also provides for procedural rights and safeguards which Member States must provide, especially if they seek to exclude an individual on the grounds of public policy, public security or public health:

• A migrant is entitled to remain in the host Member State pending a decision either to grant or refuse a residence permit. A decision to this effect should be taken no later than six months from the date of application for the permit (Article 5 of the Directive);

• An individual should be informed of the reasons a decision to bar him from a state was taken, unless this would threaten State security (Article 6 and *Rutili* [1975]); and

• The principle of natural justice in regard to appeal against decisions of immigration authorities is contained in Articles 8 and 9 (*Santillo* [1980] and *Gallagher* [1994]).

11. FREEDOM OF ESTABLISHMENT AND THE RIGHT TO SUPPLY AND RECEIVE SERVICES

Freedom of establishment and the provision and receipt of services are usually considered together because the right of establishment allows Member State nationals to set up business as self employed persons in another Member State. It allows them to take up *and* pursue activities in a host Member State without discrimination on the grounds of nationality. These two rights however, are not identical. Article 49 (ex Article 52) relating to services gives a *temporary* right lasting only as long as the services are provided and only if the provisions in Article 43 (ex Article 59) on the right of establishment, a *permanent* right, do not apply (*Gebhard* [1995]). These rights apply both to natural persons (individuals) and legal persons (companies). Article 48 applies the same rights to companies formed under the law of one of the Member States, with their registered or head office within the Community. This freedom also covers the right of so-called "secondary establishment" in another Member State, meaning the right to set up a branch or subsidiary of an existing firm or company in another state.

Some Treaty provisions relating to the freedom of establishment are similar to those already set out for workers, for example:

- Article 45 of the Treaty exempts any activities which are connected, even on an occasional basis, with the exercise of official authority (*Reyners* [1974]). This is similar to the public service exception for workers in Article 39(4).
- There is also a similar right to that in Regulation 1251/70 to remain after retirement for individuals who have established themselves in business with their families under Directive 75/34.
- The right of establishment and the right to provide (and receive) services are not absolute. Article 46(1) provides for derogations on the grounds of public policy, public security and public health which are elaborated in Directive 64/221 above (*Calfa* [1999]).
- Directive 73/148 covers rights for self-employed persons and their families to enter and leave the host state for the purpose of establishing themselves or providing or receiving services. In the case of establishment, a residence permit valid for a period of not less than five years, automatically renewable, shall be issued. In the cases, of services, the right is granted solely for the period during which the service is provided.
- There is no exact equivalent to Regulation 1612/68 which means there are no "social and tax advantages" as there would have been under Article 7(2) of that Regulation.
- Article 43 has direct effect (*Reyners* [1974]) as does Article 49 (*Van Binsbergen* [1974]).

- Nationals of a third country, although residing lawfully in a Member State, may not rely on the Treaty provisions to establish themselves in another Member State (*Razanatsimba* [1977]). Similarly, the right to provide services is limited to EU citizens already established in a Member State.
- Similar to the case of *Saunders* concerning the free movement of workers, provisions on the freedom of establishment do not apply to situations which are internal to one Member State (*Jagerskiold* [1999]).

THE RIGHT OF ESTABLISHMENT

Article 43 provides that

> "Within the framework of the provisions set out below, restrictions on the freedom of establishment of nationals of a Member State in the territory of another Member State shall be prohibited. Such prohibition shall also apply to restrictions on the setting up of agencies, branches, subsidiaries by nationals of any Member State established in the territory of any Member State.
>
> Freedom of establishment shall include the right to take up and pursue activities as self-employed persons and to set up and manage undertakings, in particular companies or firms within the meaning of the second paragraph of Art 48, under the conditions laid down for its own nationals by the law of the country where such establishment is effected, subject to the provisions of the Chapter relating to capital."

Article 48 provides that

> "Companies or firms formed in accordance with the law of a Member State and having their registered office, central administration or principal place of business within the Community shall, for the purposes of this Chapter, be treated in the same was as natural persons who are nationals of Member States.
>
> 'Companies or firms' means companies or firms constituted under civil or commercial law, including co-operative societies, and other legal persons governed by public or private law, save for those which are non-profit-making."

The Community has taken a two-pronged approach to eliminate barriers to the freedom of establishment and the provision of services:

(1) Harmonisation of Professional Qualifications

The Treaty sets out that in order to make it easier for persons to take up and pursue activities as self-employed persons, the Community would:

- Take steps to carry out a programme of secondary legislation which would ensure the mutual recognition of "diplomas, certificates and other evidence of formal qualifications"(Article 47(1)); and
- Co-ordinate national requirements governing the pursuit of non-wage-earning activities (Article 47(2)).

General Programmes for abolition of discriminatory measures both in establishment and in services were drawn up in 1961 to provide for a wide range of Directives intended to facilitate access by abolishing restrictions within the various sectors of the economy.

Directive 75/369 applied to the provisions of services as well as to the right of establishment of initially, persons such as itinerant traders, film producers, hairdressers and the providers of gas, water and electricity. These involved, in some cases, periods of academic training and practical experience and in others, a period of self-employment and a certificate of good character. Little progress was made in relation to other higher education diplomas and professional education and training although it did result in a number of Directives covering such professions such as architects, dentists and healthcare professionals. In 1985 the Commission adopted a new approach.

Directive 89/48 (Mutual Recognition of Diplomas) opened the way to a more inclusive approach. It covers the mutual recognition of diplomas without harmonisation, but includes a safeguard requiring an adaptation period in a host Member State or aptitude tests. Those who benefit from the provisions of the Directive are those who can show:

- Possession of a diploma indicating that the holder has the professional qualifications required for the taking up or pursuit of a regulated profession in one of the Member States in a self-employed capacity or as an employed person;
- Completion of a post-secondary course of at least three years' duration, or of an equivalent duration part-time, at a university or establishment of higher education or another establishment of similar level; and
- Where appropriate, that the holder of the diploma has successfully completed the professional training required in addition to the post-secondary course.

Directive 92/51 was adopted dealing with areas of professional education and training but which did not fall within Directive 89/48 as the persons involved had not completed diplomas or training for three years. As with the former Directive the host state may require the diploma holder to complete an adaptation period of not more than three years or to take an aptitude test.

Directive 93/16 was adopted to facilitate the free movement of doctors and the mutual recognition of their formal qualifications and diplomas and covers the knowledge, understanding and experience that a doctor had gained during his training period.

With particular regard to the difficulties encountered by lawyers who had to undergo an aptitude test, Directive 98/5 was adopted to make it easier for lawyers to practise in other Member States. Not all Member States enthusiastically took on board the requirement to enact this into domestic law. In *Commission v France (re Lawyers)* [2002] the Court held that in failing to implement the provisions of the Directive the French government fell short of its obligations under the Treaty.

In March 2002, the Commission proposed a new Directive for the recognition of professional qualifications, the aim of which is to have a consolidated version of the law in the field of mutual recognition of professional qualifications (COM (2002) 119 Final). It is anticipated that this will enter into force during 2005.

(2) Caselaw on the Principle of Non-discrimination

Because there is no equivalent to Regulation 1612/68, and so no "social or tax advantages" the Court has construed Article 43 in such a way as to outlaw national measures which give certain social or tax advantages to nationals (*CPM Meeusen v Hoofddirectie Van De Informatie Beheer Groep* [1999]), or to companies having their principal establishment in that Member State (*ICI v Colmer* [1998]), and which discriminate directly or indirectly against non-national natural or legal persons. Similar caselaw has excluded discrimination with regard to the provision of services.

The Court has stated that the prohibition of discrimination is concerned with the rules relating to the various facilities which are needed in order to pursue an occupation. So by applying the principle of non discrimination where harmonisation has not taken place in a particular profession, it has been possible to invoke Articles 12, 43 and 49 to challenge traditional rules which discriminate against persons or companies from other Member States.

Both direct and indirect discrimination are prohibited. The Court has not hesitated to invoke Article 12 to strike down national rules either in the form of discriminatory nationality or residence requirements (*Steinhauser v City of Biarritz* [1985] and *Commission v Italy (re Housing Aid)* [1988]).

The caselaw of the Court has also clarified the qualifications required for professionals to be able to practise in other Member States:

- If a person has already obtained what was recognised, professionally and academically as an equivalent qualification and had satisfied the necessary training requirements, there should be no obstacle to his admission to a professional body in another Member State (*Thieffry v Conseil de l'Ordre des Avocats à la Cour de Paris* [1977]).
- In *Commission v Luxembourg (re Access to the Medical Profession)* in 1992, the Court ruled that formalities necessary to become a member of a professional body must fulfil four criteria in order to be justified:
  (a) they must apply without distinction to nationals and non-nationals;
  (b) they must be justified by imperative requirements in the general interest;
  (c) they must be suitable for the objective which they pursue; and
  (d) they must not go beyond what is necessary to attain that objective.
- In *Vlassopoulou* [1991], it was held that national authorities must consider any education or training received which is indicated by the qualification and to contrast that with the knowledge and skills required by the domestic qualification. If they are equivalent, then the Member State must recognise the qualification. If they are not considered equivalent, then they must go on to consider the knowledge or training received by the applicant through study or experience, which may be sufficient to make up for what was lacking in the formal qualification. (The decision in this case whereby a Member State is required to carry out a comparative examination of diplomas was incorporated in Directive 99/42 clarifying the rules on the Recognition of Qualifications).

FREEDOM TO PROVIDE SERVICES

Article 49 deals with the provision of services as set out in Article 50. "Services" under the Treaty are those provided in one Member State for a person in another Member State.

Article 49 provides that:

"Within the framework of the provisions set out below, restrictions on freedom to provide services within the Community shall be prohibited in respect of nationals of Member States who are established in a State of the Community other than that of the person for whom the services are intended".

Article 50 provides that:

"Services shall be considered to be 'services' within the meaning of this Treaty where they are normally provided for remuneration, insofar as they are not governed by the provisions relating to freedom of movement for goods, capital and persons. 'Services' shall in particular include:

(a) activities of an industrial character
(b) activities of a commercial character
(c) activities of craftsmen
(d) activities of the professions

Without prejudice to the provisions of the Chapter relating to the right of establishment, the person providing a service, may, in order to do so, temporarily pursue his activity in the State where the service is provided, under the same conditions as are imposed by that State on its own nationals."

Again the Court has played a major part in clarifying the scope of the Treaty provisions, in particular the prohibition of discriminatory measures by Member States.

In *H.M. Customs & Excise v Schindler* [1994], the Court examined the meaning of "services". Schindler was the agent of state lotteries in Germany who sent letters from the Netherlands to the UK enclosing invitations to play the German lotteries. The Court held that the letters were not goods but services in that they were provided for remuneration and offered in another Member State.

Beneficiaries of both the right of establishment and the freedom to provide services include Community nationals as well as companies formed under the law of one of the Member States. In *Commission v Germany (re Insurance Services)* [1987], the Court held that an enterprise would be regarded as an establishment rather than a provider of services if there was no branch or agency within the Community but only an office managed by an independent person authorised to act on a permanent basis.

Van Binsbergen [1974], concerned the representation in Court of a Dutch national who was not allowed by national rules to have his legal adviser continue to represent him when the legal adviser moved to Belgium. In this case the Court set out the test of necessity and ruled that a residential qualification in a properly qualified person is not a legitimate condition of exercising that profession unless it is necessary to ensure the observance of professional rules of conduct.

In *Gebhard* [1995], the Court gave further guidance on the compatibility of national rules with the Treaty and reiterated the four criteria set out in *Commission v Luxembourg (re Access to the Medical Profession)* [1992], which were considered under freedom of establishment, above. In other words, where national measures restrict one of the Treaty's fundamental freedoms they must be non-discriminatory, be able to be justified in the general interest, be objectively necessary and in proportion to their objective.

In *Bickel and Franz* [1998], an Italian refusal to use the German language in criminal proceedings for non-German speaking Community nationals staying in Italy was unjustified with regard to the objective pursued and would constitute discrimination.

The concept of services also extends to the recipients of services. Although the Treaty makes no express reference to the receipt of services, Directive 73/148 in Article 1(b) sets out that there are to be no restrictions on

> "(a) nationals of a Member State who are established or who wish to establish themselves in another Member State in order to pursue activities as self-employed persons or who wish to provide services in that state; and
> (b) nationals of Member States wishing to go to another Member State as recipients of services."

In *Luisi and Carbone v Ministero del Tesoro* [1984], the Court held that the freedom to provide services includes the freedom for a national of another Member State to receive services under the same conditions as nationals of the host state. The principle of non-discrimination applies (*Cowan v Trésor Public* [1989]).

In *Commission v Italy (re Museum Charges)* [2003], Italian legislation on preferential rates for entry to national museums allowed only to Italian nationals and persons aged over 60 or 65 years resident within the area, was ruled as infringing the principles of free movement of services and non-discrimination.

As regards education, in *Gravier v City of Liège* [1985], a French national challenged the Belgian fee for a vocational course as discriminatory and constituting an obstacle to her Community right to vocational education. This was followed in 1988 by *Blaizot* establishing that all courses save those intended to improve the general education of students rather than prepare them for employment, are considered as vocational courses. The entitlement to loans and grants, however, is still only available to workers and their families as "social and tax advantages" under Regulation 1612/68.

12. CITIZENSHIP AND THE FREE MOVEMENT OF PERSONS

Since its creation in the Treaty on European Union, the title on Citizenship in Articles 17 to 22 of the EC Treaty now sets out that "Citizenship of the Union is hereby established. Every person holding the nationality of a Member State shall be a citizen of the Union. Citizenship of the Union shall complement and not replace national citizenship". Further, the Treaty sets out that nationals of the Member States have four specific rights:

- To move freely and reside in the territory of Member States;
- To vote and stand as a candidate in local and European Parliament elections in the Member State of residence (not of nationality);
- To protection, in a non-EU country in which the citizen's own Member State is not represented, by the diplomatic or consular authorities of any other Member State; and
- To petition the European Parliament and to apply to the European Ombudsman and to receive a reply in the citizen's own language.

The wording of the Treaty indicated that no new free movement rights for persons were to be brought into being, but solely attached the existing rights—with all their qualifications and derogations—to the new concept of citizenship. Although the exact rights of citizens were unclear, it was not long before cases arrived before the European Courts in which citizenship was a central issue:

- *Uecker and Jacquet* [1997] — citizenship was not intended to extend the scope of the Treaty to cover internal situations with no link to Community law
- *Martinez Sala* [1998] — an Spanish national living in Germany not falling within the Community definition of "a worker" (*i.e.* not carrying out economic activity) and thus not falling within the personal scope of the legal provisions was still entitled to equal treatment in relation to welfare as she came within the material scope of these benefits
- *Grzelczyk* [2001] — a French student in Belgium again, not a "worker" in the Community sense and thus not entitled to benefits was considered to have been discriminated against contrary to Article 12 of the Treaty *in conjunction* with the Treaty provisions on citizenship
- *Baumbast* [2002] — a citizen of the Union who no longer enjoyed a right of residence in a host Member State possessed a fundamental right to move and reside freely within the Union, subject to limitations and conditions laid down elsewhere in Community law. Such limitations must be exercised in accordance with the principle of proportionality, may not be arbitrary nor must they deprive the residence rights endowed of their substantive content.

With the *Baumbast* case came the recognition by the Court that Article 18 was directly effective and therefore could be relied on to provide rights which an individual could enforce through local courts.

Reform of the Rules on Free Movement of Persons

A proposal for a new draft Directive on the rights of European Union citizens and their families to move and reside freely within the Territory of the Member States was presented by the Commission in 2003 (COM (2003) 199 final). It is anticipated that two Regulations and nine Directives will be consolidated into one Directive, with the following being repealed:

- Articles 10 and 11 of Regulation 1612/68 on workers' families;
- Directive 64/221, derogations on the grounds of public policy, security and health, as amended by Directive 75/35;
- Directive 68/360 on abolition of restrictions on free movement and residence of workers and their families;
- Directive 73/148 on abolitions of restrictions on establishment and the provision of services;
- Directive 75/34 on the right to remain for the self-employed;
- Directive 90/364 on rights of residence for those not falling into other categories;
- Directive 90/365 on rights of residence for retirees; and
- Directive 93/96 on rights of residence for students.

The objective of the new legislation is to encourage citizens to exercise their right of free movement by reducing formalities, amending the definition of those to be included in the "family" and limiting derogations.

The draft legislation proposes that short stays of up to six months will be allowed on production of an identity document. Those wishing to stay for more than six months will be allowed to do so if they are engaged in economic activity *or* have sufficient resources not to be a burden on the host State *or* are following vocational training as a student *or* are a family member of the preceding categories of person the draft Directive envisages that death or divorce will not affect the rights of family members, with permanent residency being made available to all after a four-year period of residency. Equal treatment with host State nationals will also be ensured except in the area of social security.

---

13. EQUAL PAY AND TREATMENT

EQUAL PAY

Among the most important provisions of the Treaty relating to equal pay were those contained in Article 119 (now Article 141) of the Treaty. Its original provisions have been expanded by the Treaty of Amsterdam though its underlying principles remain the same. It relates to the fundamental principle of equal pay for male and female workers for equal work (or work of equal value). The object including such provisions was not only as it first appeared, for social reasons but its underlying rationale—since it dealt originally only with pay rather than all discrimination based on sex—was in keeping with the other economic provisions of the Treaty. It would therefore prevent Member States from deriving any competitive advantage over those who already had equal pay legislation, notably France. However, the Court later was to declare that this Article was intended, by common action, to ensure social progress and to seek the constant improvement of working conditions. Consequently, the following Directives to elaborate on the basic Treaty principles have been adopted:

* Equal Pay Directive 75/117;
* Equal Treatment Directive 76/207;
* Equal treatment for men and women in matters of social security—Directive 79/7;
* Equal treatment between self-employed men and women and on the protection of self-employed women during pregnancy and motherhood—Directive 86/613;
* Pregnancy and Maternity Directive 92/85;
* Working Time Directive 93/104;
* Framework agreement on parental leave—Directive 96/34;
* Equal Treatment in Occupation Pensions Directive 96/97 (amending Directive 86/378);
* Burden of Proof in Sex Discrimination Cases (if a claimant has established discrimination, it shall be for the employer to prove that there has been no breach of the principle of equal treatment) Directive 97/80 (amended by Directive 98/52); and
* Framework Agreement on part-time work—Directive 97/81.

(1) Equal Pay
Article 141 has direct effect—not only vertical in that a Member State is bound by the Treaty provisions towards its citizens, but horizontal so that individuals such as private companies are bound to comply with its provisions in their treatment of employees (*Defrenne v SABENA* [1976]).

The Community has thus endeavoured to give Article 141 as wide a scope as possible. It has extended the concept of "discrimination" to cover not only direct but also indirect discrimination. Indirect discrimination may arise as a result of employment practices which seem to be based on neutral considerations but which in fact have the practical effect of putting one sex at a disadvantage towards the other. This type of discrimination is not necessarily unlawful if it can be proved that it is capable of objective justification (*Rinner-Kuhn* [1989]).

The first two paragraphs of Article 141 state:

"Each Member State shall ensure that the principle of equal pay for male and female workers for equal work or work of equal value is applied.

For the purpose of this Article, 'pay' means the ordinary basic or minimum wage or salary and any other consideration, whether in cash or in kind, which the worker receives directly or indirectly, in respect of his employment, from his employer.

Equal pay without discrimination based on sex means:

(a) that pay for the same work at piece rates shall be calculated on the basis of the same unit of measurement;

(b) that pay for work at time rates shall be the same for the same job."

Notwithstanding the definition within the Treaty, the notion of "pay" raised questions as to the exact scope of the provision. A series of cases has established that "pay" can include:

* Concessionary travel facilities after retirement (*Garland v BREL* [1982]);
* Statutory Sick pay (*Rinner-Kuhn v FWW* [1989]);
* Private occupational pension schemes (*Worringham and Humphries v Lloyds Bank Ltd* [1981] and *Barber v Guardian Royal Exchange* [1990]);
* Indemnities paid under statute to workers attending day-release training courses (*Bötel* [1992]);
* Severance pay negotiated under a collective bargaining agreement (*Kowalski* [1990]); and
* Maternity pay (*Gillespie v Northern Ireland Health and Social Services Board* [1996]).

Directive 75/117 was introduced to clarify the position of workers who, for example, carry out the same work but where one job is paid less than another where lesser skills and qualifications are required; or where a woman is paid less than a man doing a job that, although different, is alleged to be of comparable economic worth. It concerns equal pay for work of equal value. The Directive requires Member States to set up methods whereby an evaluation of comparability may be undertaken at the request of an employee. Since the Treaty of Amsterdam this duty is provided for within the text of Article 141 itself (see above).

(2) Equal Treatment

Although equal treatment of men and women is not mentioned in the Treaty, its scope has been extended through a series of Directives (see above) seen as a necessary corollary to the Equal Pay Directive. In particular, the Equal Treatment Directive 76/207 elaborates on the principles of equality of access to employment including promotion, to vocational training and as regards working conditions. Many of its provisions have since fallen into the scope of the Pregnancy and Maternity Directive 92/85.

The Equal Treatment Directive also provides for strictly defined derogations from its provisions under certain circumstances. Article 2(2) of the Directive, for example allows exemption from the equal treatment principle for activities for which the sex of the worker constitutes a determining factor (*Sirdar* [1999]). In *Kalanke v Freie Hansestadt Bremen* [1995] the Court limited the interpretation of the derogation in Article 2(4) and held that national rules to give automatic priority to women candidates where they were under-represented in the event that male and female candidates for a job were equally qualified, went beyond the bounds of promoting equal opportunity. The scope of the judgment was clarified in *Marschall v Land Nordrhein-Westfalen* [1997] where it was held that providing an objective assessment taking account of all the criteria specific to individual candidates was made, such positive action would be acceptable as long as the criteria themselves did not discriminate against women. The test would be that preference for a women would be displaced where reasons specific to an individual male candidate tilted the balance in his favour.

The scope for measures in favour of the disadvantaged sex in employment has been extended with the Treaty of Amsterdam. The aim of gender equality is covered in Articles 2 and in Article 3(2) of the Treaty (as amended) which sets out "[i]n all the activities referred to in this Article, the Community shall aim to eliminate inequalities, and to promote equality, between men and women". Article 13 entitles the Commission to take initiative to combat discrimination. In addition, the fourth paragraph of Article 141 now reads:

> "With a view to ensuring full equality in practice between men and women in working life, the principle of equal treatment shall not prevent any Member State from maintaining or adopting measures providing for specific advantages in order to make it easier for the under-represented sex to pursue a vocational activity or to prevent or compensate for disadvantages in professional careers."

14. COMPETITION LAW AND POLICY

The tasks of the Community are set out in Article 2 of the Treaty and include the promotion of a "harmonious and balanced and sustainable development of economic activities". The primary means by which this was originally to be achieved was by progressive abolition of all hindrances to the free movement of goods. However, whilst recognising that dismantling Member States' barriers against competition from goods from other Member States was necessary to create a Common Market, this would not on its own be sufficient if businesses were allowed to distort the market to their advantage and to the disadvantage of competitors and consumers. Article 3 sets out how the Community's tasks are to be achieved by activities such as creating and maintaining "a system ensuring that competition in the internal market is not distorted" (Article 3(g)). Two fundamental objectives of the Community— market integration and the promotion of competitive markets within the Community itself—are thus incorporated within the Treaty.

The objectives of European competition policy incorporate equality or fairness. The Treaty Articles relating to State Aid for example, ensure that Member States do not favour their own national industries by providing monetary or fiscal advantages to them alone and not to competitors from other Member States. Any such subsidies must be compatible with the provisions as set out in the Treaty.

The Community is also a major world trading bloc. Because the size and sophistication of the companies within the Community who are seeking to enter this global market can differ markedly, it is in the Community's interest that economic integration proceeds as speedily and efficiently as possible to bring prosperity to its manufacturing and service industries. Competition policy therefore also seeks to create and maintain a healthy competitive economic base and in particular to encourage the growth of small and medium-sized enterprises (SMEs) which are economically valuable both to their own Member State and to the Community as a whole, as well as encouraging an "enterprise culture" within Europe. Legal certainty within the small-business community is also recognised as essential to a competitive market.

The importance of protecting consumers—whether as retailers acquiring goods for re-sale or users of the end product—from the effects of anti-competitive conduct is also recognised. The Treaty sets out that consumers should receive a fair share of the benefit of any agreements made between businesses. This can range from a greater variety of products, improved service or guaranteed facilities to more retail outlets for the goods in question.

By promoting a healthy competitive culture within Europe and thus encouraging efficient production and effective allocation of goods and services between member states and as part of a wider market, efficiency is also recognised as being one of the major aims of competition policy. However, Community competition rules are not designed to promote efficiency at all costs. If this were so, it would protect the most efficient companies at all times and eliminate small and less efficient firms from potential new markets. In turn this would have an adverse effect on the objectives of integration, competitiveness and fairness. What the Community is concerned with is the structural behaviour of undertakings in a market and eliminating barriers to entry for new and potential entrants; legal, fiscal, historical and cultural barriers. Rather, the competition rules are concerned with the control of dominance within a market and the methods by which undertakings acquire and hold on to market power.

Because competition policy is dynamic, existing within an intensely economic and political environment, it has evolved from minimal provisions in the original EEC Treaty, through the caselaw of the Court of Justice and the developing institutional awareness of the Commission into a mature and comprehensive system of rules applying throughout an increasing number of industrial and service sectors of the Community's economy.

Thus European Community competition rules seek to contribute to the promotion of market integration, to the strengthening of consumer protection and to the maximisation of economic performance within Member States. Competition policy is therefore central to the establishment and maintenance of an open market economy, enabling business and industry throughout the European Community to compete effectively and efficiently in the global arena.

The main provisions of the Treaty relating to competition policy are Article 81 (ex Article 85) which aims to control anti-competitive practices such as agreements which restrict or distort competition and Article 82 (ex Article 86) preventing large undertakings from abusing a dominant position.

Certain forms of anti-competitive conduct may infringe both Articles (*Hoffmann La Roche* [1979]). These two Treaty Articles complement others to control government intervention aimed at sheltering national industries, such as those found in Articles 87 to 89 (ex Articles 92 to 94) relating to State Aid and Article 86 (ex Article 90) covering publicly controlled undertakings.

These are supplemented by secondary legislation to reinforce and expand the outline Treaty provisions, notably Regulation 4064/89 covering mergers (from May 2004, to be replaced by Regulation 139/2004).

Not only do the competition rules apply to companies operating anti-competitively within Member States but also to parent companies located outside the EC and their European subsidiaries (*Istituto Chemioterapico Italiano SpA and Commercial Solvents Corporation v Commission* [1973]), and to agreements made between non-EC companies if their practices were implemented in the Community (*Ahlström (A) Oy v Commission* [1993]).

Through Directorate-General IV (DGIV) which is responsible for competition policy, the Commission plays a key role in the enforcement of the Community's rules on competition within the Member States and can instigate proceedings for infringements of competition law. In accordance with Regulation 17/62 (to be replaced in May 2004 by Regulation 1/2003) the Commission has extensive powers of investigation and enforcement.

Infringement of the competition rules may incur financial penalties. The Commission is entitled to levy fines of up to 10 per cent of the turnover for the preceding financial year whichever is the greater (including all group turnover), for intentional or negligent infringement of Articles 81 and 82. It may therefore be assumed that the deterrent effect of disregarding the Community's competition rules is considerable. In fixing the amount of the fine, the Commission will have regard both to the gravity and duration of the infringement

Article 81(1) and (2) and Article 82 have direct effect (*BRT and SABAM* [1974]).

ARTICLE 81

Article 81 prohibits collusive behaviour between undertakings which would have an effect on competition and affect trade between Member States. The Article itself is in three parts. Article 81(1) sets out the prohibited conduct, Article 81(2) the consequences of indulging in such anti-competitive behaviour and Article 81(3) allows the Commission to grant exemptions under certain conditions. It reads as follows:

"(1) The following shall be prohibited as incompatible with the common market: all agreements between undertakings, decisions by associations of undertakings and concerted practices which may affect trade between Member States and which have as their object or effect the prevention, restriction or distortion of competition within the common market, and in particular those which—
(a) directly or indirectly fix purchase or selling prices of any other trading conditions;

(b) limit or control production, markets, technical development, or investment;

(c) share markets or sources of supply;

(d) apply dissimilar conditions to equivalent transactions with other trading parties, thereby placing them at a competitive disadvantage;

(e) make the conclusion of contracts subject to acceptance by the other parties of supplementary obligations which, by their nature or according to commercial usage, have no connection with the subject of such contracts.

(2) Any agreements or decisions prohibited pursuant to this Article shall be automatically void.

(3) The provisions of paragraph 1 may, however, be declared inapplicable in the case of:

—any agreement or category of agreements between undertakings;

—any decision or category of decisions by associations of undertakings;

—any concerted practice or category of concerted practices,

which contributes to improving the production or distribution of goods or to promoting technical or economic progress, while allowing consumers a fair share of the resulting benefit, and which does not:

(a) impose on the undertakings concerned restrictions which are not indispensable to the attainment of these objectives;

(b) afford such undertakings the possibility of eliminating competition in respect of a substantial part of the products in question.

"Agreement"

The meaning of the term "agreement", within the context of Article 81(1) is wider than simply a contractual obligation, whether written or oral. Even an arrangement between parties that is not legally binding may constitute an agreement (*Re Polypropylene* [1988]), as does a "gentleman's agreement" enforceable by arbitration (*ACF Chemiefarma* [1970]).

Agreements may be "horizontal", that is between companies at the same level of trade or industry (the parties are all manufacturers, distributors, retailers, etc.,) or "vertical", between companies at different levels of a trade or industry (a manufacturer with a distributor, a wholesaler with a retailer and so on). Both types of agreement may fall within the prohibitions of Article 81(1) (*Société Technique Minière* [1966]).

Unilateral action taken by a manufacturer to refuse the supply of certain goods to its distributors has also been defined as "an agreement" (*Ford Werke v Commission* [1985]). The Court ruled that this ostensibly one-sided arrangement was so closely connected to a system of individual agreements between the manufacturer and its distributors that the unilateral action was part of the whole contractual framework between the manufacturer and its distributors.

"Undertakings"

In the absence of any precise definition within the Treaty, the Court has interpreted the concept of an undertaking widely to include any economic entity, company, partnership, sole trader or group of companies, whether providing goods or services, commercial or cultural, public or private. Examples of undertakings range from opera singers (*RAI/Unitel* [1978]), to port authorities (*Merci Convenzionale Porto di Genova v Siderurgica Gabrielle SpA* [1991]). The fact that an entity is state-owned or state-financed and provides a service normally provided by the state does not prevent it from being considered an undertaking if it provides services of "general economic interest" (*Job Centre Coop* [1998]).

The Court will also regard as one undertaking, companies that are ostensibly legally separate such as parent companies and their subsidiaries but which in fact are linked through ownership and management agreements (*Viho Europe BV v Commission* [1996]). In these cases, the Court applies the "economic entity" principle, judging both companies to be one undertaking when a sufficient degree of control is exercised by the parent to leave no room for independent management by the subsidiary. Agreements made between the two will then be considered as an allocation of functions (*Béguelin* [1971]).

"Decisions by associations of undertakings"

An "association of undertakings" refers to a trade association, federation or syndicate. An example of a prohibited activity would include the recommendation of prices even if such recommended prices were claimed to be non-binding (*Vereeniging van Cementhandelaren v Commission* [1972]), or a non-binding code of conduct (*Publishers' Association v Commission* [1992]).

"Concerted practices"

Where two or more undertakings co-operate—no matter how informally—on some co-ordinated anti-competitive practice, such as price fixing or refusal to supply, such activities may result in investigation under Article 81(1). Even though no formal agreement may exist between the undertakings involved, the Court has nevertheless defined "concerted practice" as

> "a form of co-ordination between enterprises that has not yet reached the point where it is a contract in the true sense of the word but which, in practice, consciously substitutes practical co-operation for the risks of competition" (*ICI v Commission (Dyestuffs)* [1972]).

Although evidence of collusive practices between companies can be difficult to establish, apparently inter-related behaviour such as price rises or other parallel conduct in itself will not necessarily constitute proof of a concerted practice (*Åhlstrom (A) Oy v Commission* [1993]).

In order to determine whether any agreements reached by undertakings fall within the prohibition laid down by Article 81(1) of the Treaty, the Court has regard to three distinct elements:

- Whether the object or effect of the agreement is to restrict competition;

- Whether such restriction applies to an appreciable extent within the common market; and
- Whether the agreement may affect trade between Member States.

"Object or effect"

The Court has ruled that there is no need to take account of the practical effect of an agreement once it appears that it has as its object the prevention, restriction or distortion of competition (*Société Technique Minière* [1966]). However, if the object of an agreement is clearly not anti-competitive, consideration will be then be given to its effect (*Delimitis v Henninger Bräu* [1991]). Examination of the agreement within its economic and legal context will then take place to reach a conclusion as to whether the effect of the practice breaches Article 81(1) on the basis of:

- The nature or quantity of the products to which the agreement relates;
- The position and importance of the parties in the relevant product and geographical markets;
- Whether the agreement is isolated or part of a network;
- The severity of the restriction; and
- The existence of patents, trademarks or other intellectual property.

"the prevention, restriction or distortion of competition within the common market"

The list of agreements capable of distorting the structure of the market is set out in Article 81(1) but is by no means exhaustive. The essential element is that collusion between undertakings capable of distorting the structure of the market has taken place. Distortion can also arise through the existence of an agreement between two undertakings and a third, which is not party to the original agreement (*Consten and Grundig v Commission* [1966]).

"to an appreciable extent"

This is known as the *de minimis* doctrine. Even though the wording of the Treaty indicates that any effect on competition and trade between Member States is sufficient to trigger the application of Article 81, the Court confirmed early on that this must be "appreciable" (*Völk v Vervaecke* [1969]). Shortly afterwards, in the early 1970s, the Commission clarified this judgment by publishing a guidance Notice on Agreements of Minor Importance quantifying the *de minimis* threshold. The most recent Notice ([2001] O.J. C368/13) provides that agreements concerning goods or services will not be considered under Article 81(1) if the market share of all the participating undertakings in the relevant markets does not exceed:

- A 10 per cent threshold where the agreement is made between undertakings operating at the same level of production (horizontal agreements); or
- A 15 per cent threshold where the agreement is made between undertakings operating at different levels of production (vertical agreements); and
- Small and medium sized enterprises (SMEs) are considered by the Commission to be rarely capable of appreciably affecting trade between

Member States. The Commission considers that agreements between SMEs therefore generally fall outside the scope of Article 81(1).

"which may affect trade between Member States"

If an agreement is not capable of affecting trade between Member States—actually or potentially—Article 81 will not apply. For the agreement to fall within Article 81, it is sufficient that the agreement is likely to affect trade, even in the future.

If an agreement is made, *the effects of which are confined to the territory of a single Member State*, it does not fall under Article 81, but is governed by the national legal order (*Hugin Cash Registers v Commission* [1979]).

Exemptions

Although an agreement has, or is intended to have an anti-competitive effect, it may be subject to an exemption from the prohibitions in Article 81(1). In an attempt to balance the economic interests of undertakings, consumers and the Community itself with the desire to avoid unnecessary restrictions on business enterprise, Article 81(3) provides for some agreements, decisions or concerted practices which, although they reduce competition, may also have beneficial consequences which outweigh their restrictive effects; which contribute towards improving the production or distribution of goods; or to promoting technical or economic progress whilst allowing consumers a fair share in the benefits of such arrangements. As well as possessing these "positive" attributes, the arrangements made must also abide by two "negative" conditions. First, they must be no more restrictive than absolutely necessary in order to achieve the undertaking's apparent objective and secondly, they must not give the undertakings the opportunity to eliminate any competitors.

Until May 2004, the Commission has exclusive jurisdiction to grant exemptions from the prohibitions laid down in Article 81(1). At that time, new Regulation 1/2003 will come into effect. Its aim is to strengthen competition in the Community and will extend to national competition authorities and courts the power to apply Community competition law in full. The Commission will therefore no longer have the sole power to apply Article 81(3). Where agreements, decisions and concerted practices have effects that are incompatible with Article 81(3) the Commission and the competition authorities of the Member State will have the power to deal with them.

Block Exemptions

These allow undertakings to make their own assessment as to whether or not the agreement in question falls within one of the block exemptions and draft their agreements to comply with its requirements. They may then treat the agreement as valid and enforceable. If it does not, then application must be made to the Commission or, under certain circumstances, the competition authorities of the Member States for an individual exemption. Even if an agreement falls within a block exemption this does not necessarily guarantee immunity. Block exemptions to date have included:

- Motor Vehicle Vertical Agreements (Regulation 1400/2002);
- Technology Transfer Agreements (Regulation 240/96);
- Exclusive Distribution and Purchasing, and Franchising Agreements (Regulation 2790/99);
- Specialisation Agreements (Regulation 2658/2000);
- Research and Development Agreements (Regulation 2659/2000); and
- Insurance Agreements (Regulation 358/2003).

Individual Exemptions
These depend on compliance with the requirements of Article 81(3). Exemptions may be granted only for specific periods, conditions may be attached and the exemption may be revoked or renewed. Because of the workload of the Commission, it sometimes issues a "comfort letter" stating that in its opinion, the agreement does not infringe Article 81(1). A comfort letter does not have the binding effect of a Commission decision allowing an undertaking to challenge it under Article 230 or to bind national courts (*SA Lancôme v ETOS BV* [1980]). It is simply an administrative letter allowing an undertaking to rely on the Commission not taking further action. The file is then closed, although it may be reopened if legal, material or factual circumstances change or misrepresentation has taken place.

Agreements and decisions infringing Article 81(1) which do not qualify for exemption under Article 81(3) are automatically void from their inception under Article 81(2). However, if it is possible to sever any offending clauses it is not necessary for the whole agreement to be considered void (*Consten and Grundig* [1966]). This would be for a national court to determine.

ARTICLE 82

Undertakings that find their ability to form anti-competitive agreements curtailed under Article 81 may seek to merge into a single entity to frustrate the competition rules. Article 82 controls companies seeking to evade prohibition by these means. In order to control undertakings which hold such powerful economic positions that they are not only able to dominate the market in which they operate, but derive unfair advantages and can eliminate their competitors, Article 82 sets out the following:

> "Any abuse by one or more undertakings of a dominant position within the common market or in a substantial part of it shall be prohibited as incompatible with the common market in so far as it may affect trade between Member States. Such abuse may, in particular, consist in:
> (a) directly or indirectly imposing unfair purchase or selling prices or unfair trading conditions;
> (b) limiting production, markets or technical development to the prejudice of consumers;
> (c) applying dissimilar conditions to equivalent transactions with other trading parties, thereby placing them at a competitive disadvantage;
> (d) making the conclusion of contracts subject to acceptance by the other parties of supplementary obligations which, by their nature or according to commercial usage, have no connection with the subject of such contracts."

Unlike Article 81 which deals with agreements between one or more undertakings, Article 82 deals with the abuse of a dominant position by (usually) a single company. Although the prohibited conduct set out in Article 82 closely corresponds to the examples set out within Article 81(1), again, these are not exhaustive. The caselaw of the Court indicates that wider instances of exploitative conduct than those set out in the Treaty will be prohibited.

There are no exemptions in respect of Article 82. The prohibition is absolute.

Article 82 comes into operation when three factors exist:

- A dominant position is held by one or more undertakings either within the common market or within a substantial part of it;
- That dominant position is abused; and
- And—as with Article 81—abuse in question affects trade between Member States.

Once again, in the absence of detailed definition within the Treaty, the caselaw of the Court defines the terms.

"Dominant position"
In order to establish dominance, it must be established that the undertaking in question was dominant in a particular market. This is usually taken to mean that the undertaking concerned "has the power to behave to an appreciable extent independently of its competitors, customers and ultimately of its consumers" (*United Brands v Commission* [1978]).

Relevant Market
The first objective is to define the market in which the undertaking is alleged to be dominant. In other words, it is essential to identify the "relevant market"; what products constitute it and where the geographical boundaries of this market lie.

With regard to the relevant product market, interchangeability of products is the key factor in its identification. If a consumer can easily switch to another item, it would seem that on the face of it, competition within that particular market has not been stifled and there would thus be no necessity for Commission intervention. To assess whether or not interchangeability of products exists, the Commission considers the characteristics of the commodities themselves and those of other goods that can be substituted for them. Products that only have limited interchangeability with others are not usually considered part of the relevant market (*Michelin v Commission* [1983]). From the Commission's point of view, the narrower the definition of the relevant market, the more likely it is that the undertaking will be found to be dominant in that market; while an undertaking would naturally prefer that an assessment would define the market broadly.

To evaluate the relevant geographical market, the Treaty states that Article 82 will apply to conduct "within the common market or in a substantial part of it". An assessment will look at the level of trading in one or more Member States compared to that in the Union as a whole. It is not necessary for an undertaking to carry out its activities in all Member States of the European Union; even activities in one Member State may be enough to trigger the application of Article 82 provided that these had an effect on trade between Member States (*Michelin v Commission* [1983]).

In order to render its policy and decision making more transparent and thus enable undertakings to enjoy an element of legal certainty when drawing up their agreements, acquisitions and joint ventures, in 1997 the Commission published a Notice setting out guidelines to its definition of the relevant market ([1997] O.J. C372/5).

Establishing Dominance

Once the relevant market has been evaluated, the key objective is to establish dominance of that market. Several factors are relevant to the assessment of an undertaking's dominance.

Two major cases serve to indicate not only the approach of the Commission in establishing anti-competitive conduct under Article 82, but the imprimatur of the Court of their findings. In *Hoffmann La Roche v Commission* in 1979 and *United Brands v Commission* in 1978, the Commission found that dominance would be considered:

* Where large market shares have been in place for a considerable time;
* Where the position of existing and potential competitors is taken into account;
* Where an undertaking's share of the market was appreciably in excess of its competitors;
* Where difficulties were faced by potential competitors trying to break into the market such as instances where customers are locked in to existing products and contracts; and
* Where substantial resources have been expended on product brand image and advertising.

Collective Dominance

Although most incidences of illegal abuse of a dominant position relate to the activities of a single undertaking, Article 82 condemns anti-competitive conduct by "one or more undertakings". This collective dominance usually takes place when two or more undertakings, because of the economic links between them, hold a collective dominant position on the relevant market (*Società Italiana Vetro SpA v Commission* [1992]).

Abuse

Once it has been established that an undertaking holds a dominant position in a particular market, it is necessary to determine whether or not it has abused this position. Dominance of itself is not illegal. What is prohibited is abuse of the dominant position. The Court has stated that an undertaking in a dominant position "has a special responsibility not to allow its conduct to impair undistorted competition on the common market" (*Michelin v Commission* [1983]).

It has condemned abusive practices such as:

* Excessive and discriminatory pricing (*United Brands v Commission* [1978]);

- Predatory pricing (*AKZO Chemie BV v Commission* [1991]);
- Fidelity rebates (*BPB Industries plc & British Gypsum* [1995] and *Michelin* [2003]);
- Tying-in practices (*Hoffmann La Roche v Commission* [1979] and *Hilti v Commission* [1994]); and
- Refusals to supply (*Instituto Chemioterapico Italiano SpA* and *Commercial Solvents Corporation v Commission* [1973]).

"in so far as it may affect trade between Member States"
As with Article 81 if the practice in question does not affect trade between Member States, then Article 82 will not apply. Nevertheless, for the operation of Article 82 to be triggered, it is sufficient that the conduct might affect trade even in the future (*British Leyland v Commission* [1986]).

Enforcement
Directorate-General IV of the Commission (DGIV) plays the key role in the enforcement of the competition rules. Article 85 (ex Article 89) provides that "The Commission shall ensure the application of the principles laid down in Articles 81 and 82".

The Commission may initiate enforcement proceedings on receipt of a complaint, through Members of the European Parliament, on its own account (through newspaper or trade journal reports) or—most commonly—by means of the notification procedure. Form C has been prepared by the Commission for use by complainants, but use of this is not mandatory provided that the presentation of all relevant information is complete and factually accurate. There is also a general prohibition on the disclosure of confidential information by the Commission to safeguard a complainant's identity (*Adams v Commission* [1985]).

The Commission may initiate proceedings against undertakings or their subsidiaries which are not based within the European Community but which conclude anti-competitive agreements, decisions or concerted practices which are then implemented within the Member States. This "doctrine of extraterritoriality" means that even if the parties to an agreement are not based or registered within any of the Member States, nor were the agreements in question actually concluded within the Member States, the fact that within the Community the agreements were implemented and their effects were felt is enough to bring them within the ambit of the competition rules. (*Ahlström (A) Oy v Commission* [1993]).

By the early 1990s it had become clear that effective enforcement of the competition rules was beginning to falter due mainly to the excessive workload placed upon the Commission. The acceptance of the subsidiarity principle within the Maastricht Treaty under Article 5 (ex Article 3b) also added an incentive to the Commission's decision to decentralise much of its enforcement to national competition authorities (NCAs). In turn the Member States have, for the most part, either adopted or amended their own national competition laws, holding to the principles of Articles 81 and 82. At the same time, their competition authorities have been progressively closely involved with the Commission and consequently have become more familiar with the European competition rules. In 1997, the Commission published a Notice on Co-operation with National Authorities ([1997] O.J. C313/3) setting out the special nature of the role played by national competition authorities, their expertise and knowledge of national markets. In addition, the NCAs already possessed the power through Regulation 17/62 to administer Articles 81(1) and 82 as long as the Commission had not already initiated proceedings Despite the Commission retaining jurisdiction in those cases with a "Community interest" and individual exemptions under Article 81(3), decentralisation of the administration and enforcement of European competition rules to national authorities has continued apace.

In September 2000 the Commission published a White Paper on Modernisation of the Rules implementing Articles 81 and 82 within which it set out its proposals for a Council Regulation to reform the rules on competition enforcement particularly in the light of the imminent enlargement of the Union This new Regulation 1/2003 enters into force in May 2004.

Under the new Regulation, national competition authorities will have the power to apply Articles 81 and 82. They can require an infringement to be brought to an end, order interim measures, accept commitments and impose fines, periodic penalty payments or any other penalty provided for in national law. Article 11 of the new Regulation provides for co-operation between the Commission and the national competition authorities in applying the European rules. Article 6 allows the national courts to apply Articles 81, 82 and 83 of the Treaty.

If the Commission decides there is a *prima facie* infringement, its first step is to investigate. The main powers are set out within Regulation 1/2003 as follows:

Article 18	**Requests for information** Information may be requested from the undertaking, stating the legal basis and the purpose of the request, specifying the information required, setting time-limits and penalties for supplying incorrect or misleading information and indicating the right of appeal to the Court of Justice. A copy is sent to the national competition authority
Article 19	**Power to take statements** The Commission has power to conduct interviews to collect information. Officials doing so must inform the national competition authority who may accompany Commission officials

Article 20	**The Commissions powers of inspection** The Commission has power to make "all necessary investigations into undertakings" that is, (1) to enter premises, land and means of transport; (2) to examine the books and other business records; (3) to copy and take extracts; (4) to seal the premises for the period necessary for the inspection; (5) to ask for oral explanations and record the answers. After consulting the national competition authority, and with its active assistance, the Commission requires to produce written authorisation specifying the subject matter, purpose of inspection and penalties for incomplete, incorrect or misleading answers, and the right to have the decision reviewed by the Court of Justice. The Member State shall afford necessary assistance requesting assistance of police or other enforcement authority. The national judicial authority shall ensure that coercive measures are proportional and neither arbitrary not excessive.
Article 23	**Penalties** The Commission is entitled to levy fines not exceeding one per cent of the total turnover for any undertaking that intentionally or negligently supplies misleading information, or refuses to comply with decisions requiring production of information. It may impose fines not exceeding ten per cent of its total turnover on undertakings where they likewise infringe Articles 81 or 82 (See also Commission Notice of 1997 on Guidelines on Methods of Setting Fines ([1998] O.J. C9/3), the amount

	to be determined according to the gravity and duration of the infringement.
Article 24	Periodic penalty payments may be imposed not exceeding 5 per cent of the average daily turnover
Article 27	**Hearings** Before the Commission makes a decision on the merits of a case, it shall give the undertaking concerned the opportunity of being heard on the matters under dispute. The right of defence shall be fully respected with access allowed to the Commission's file, subject to legitimate interest of undertakings in the protection of their business secrets
Article 31	**Review of the Commission's decision** The Court of Justice has unlimited jurisdiction to review decisions whereby the Commission has fixed a fine or periodic penalty payment. It may cancel, reduce or increase the amounts.

Although the Commission was previously under no duty to give advance notification of an investigation to an undertaking (*National Panasonic (UK) Ltd v Commission* [1980]), Article 20 (4) of the new Regulation sets out that the decision of the Commission to inspect an undertaking shall appoint the date on which it is to begin. Moreover, where a compulsory investigation is opposed, an undertaking's rights must also be protected by the procedural guarantees laid down by national law (*Hoechst AG v Commission* [1989]).

Compliance is enforced with the assistance of the "competent authority" in the appropriate Member State. In the UK, this is the Director General for Fair Trading who can apply for appropriate injunctions to enforce the powers of the Commission. The Commission copies all important papers to the OFT which comments on cases which raise important issues, particularly where UK interests are involved. Its representatives attend hearings in Brussels when companies make their response to the Statement of Objections issued by the Commission and they participate in an Advisory Committee on Restrictive Practices and Monopolies which considers decisions before they are made final.

Legal professional privilege may be claimed but not in respect of communications to in-house lawyers or lawyers based outside the Community. Communications to independent lawyers may be privileged if they are made after proceedings were initiated or closely linked with the subject matter of the investigation (*A M & S Europe Ltd v Commission* [1982]).

Documents acquired by the Commission during the course of its investigations will inevitably be commercially sensitive. The Commission has a general duty not to disclose information on business secrets acquired by it during the course of its investigations (*AKZO Chemie BV v Commission* [1986] and Article 28 of the Regulation).

Any information acquired as a result of Commission investigations shall only be used for the purpose of the relevant investigation although national authorities are not precluded from relying on such information when deciding whether or not to initiate national proceedings (*Direcciòn General de Defensa de la Competencia v Asociaciòn Española de Banca Privada* [1992]).

In the event of the Commission finding a breach of the competition rules, an undertaking is not obliged to admit to an infringement and is entitled to refuse to answer questions if its responses would be self-incriminating (*Orkem v Commission* [1989]).

APPENDIX 1

MAASTRICHT TREATY ON EUROPEAN UNION

(as amended by the Treaty of Amsterdam in force May 1, 1999)

Modifications to Paris Treaty (ECSC)

Modifications to Rome Treaty (Euratom)

Modifications to Rome Treaty (E.C. Treaty)

Police and Judicial Co-operation in Criminal Matters

Co-operation on Foreign and Security Policy

Cohesion Fund

General principles

Subsidiarity

New, modified and amplified competences

(EMU - Culture - Vocational Training - Consumer protection - Public Health - Trans-European Networks - Industry - Environmental protection - Economic and Social Cohesion - R & TD - Development co-operation - Visas - Asylum - Immigration- Employment - Social Policy)

Citizenship

New powers and institutions

European Parliament

Extension of positive assent and co-operation procedures
New co-decision procedure
Introduction of negative assent procedure

Court of Justice (sanctions)

Ombudsman

Appointment of Commission

Committee of the Regions

Committees of Enquiry

INDEX

Abuse of dominant position,
  abuse, 100
  collective dominance, 100
  dominant position, 98
  enforcement, 100-104
  establishing dominance, 99
  generally, 97-98
  relevant market, 99
  in so far as it may affect trade
    between Member States, 100
Annulment action, 42-47
  acts capable of being challenged,
    43
  Article 230, 42
  consequences of annulment, 47
  essential procedural requirement,
    infringement of, 46
  grounds for challenge,
    essential procedural
      requirement, infringement
      of, 46
    lack of competence, 46
  hurdles for successful claim, 42
  jurisdiction, 42
  lack of competence, 46
  right to challenge, 43-45
  time limits, 47
Assent procedure,
  European Parliament, 26-27

**Citizenship and the Free Movement
  of Persons, 89**
  Treaty on European Union, 88
Co-decision procedure,
  European Parliament, 26
Comitology, 21
Commission. *See* **European
  Commission**
Commissioners, 18
Common Market,
  effective, 4
Competition law,
  application of rules, 92
  Article 81, 93-97
    agreement, 94
    appreciable extent, 96
    block exemptions, 97
    concerted practices, 95

Competition law—*cont.*
    decisions by associations of
      undertakings, 94-95
    exemptions, 96-97
    individual exemptions, 97
    object or effect, 95
    prevention, restriction or
      distortion of competition,
      95
    prohibition, 94
    undertakings, 94
    which may affect trade
      between Member States,
      96
  Article 82, 99-106. *See also* Abuse
    of dominant position
  consumer protection, 92
  enforcement, 100-104
  generally, 91-93
  infringement of rules, 92-93
  policy objectives, 91
  role of Community, 91
  Treaty provisions, 91
Concerted practices, 93-95
Consultation procedure,
  European Parliament, 26
Consumer protection, 92
COREPER, 22
Council of Europe, 30
**Council of the European Union, 21-
  24**
  advisory committees, 22
  COREPER, 22
  establishment, 4
  voting, 22-23
Council of Ministers. *See* **Council of
  the European Union**
Court of Auditors, 30
Court of First Instance, 29
  caselaw, 15
Courts of justice,
  Court of First Instance, 29
  European Court of Justice, 27-29
    composition, 27
    functions, 28
    powers, 28
  generally, 27
  origins, 27